The Call to Ministry

The Vision of Bishop John J. Sullivan

Julie Sly

Sheed & Ward

Sheed & Ward™ is a service of The National Catholic Reporter Publishing Company.

◆

Library of Congress Cataloguing-in-Publication Data

Sly, Julie
    The call to ministry : the vision of Bishop John J. Sullivan / Julie Sly.
        p.   cm.
    ISBN 1-55612-718-9 (alk. paper)
    1. Sullivan, John J. (John Joseph), 1920-   . 2. Catholic Church—Missouri—Bishops—Biography. 3. Missouri—Church history.
    I. Title.
    BX4705.S876S48 1994
    282'.092—dc20
      [B]   94-38277
                                               CIP

◆

Published by: Sheed & Ward
               115 E. Armour Blvd.
               P.O. Box 419492
               Kansas City, MO 64141

To order, call: (800) 333-7373

Cover design by Emil Antonucci. Cover photo by Julie Sly. All photos reprinted with permission from *The Catholic Key,* Diocese of Kansas City-St. Joseph, Missouri.

Contents

Acknowledgments

THIS BOOK IS BASED LARGELY ON A SERIES OF INTERVIEWS with Bishop John Joseph Sullivan during 1993 and 1994. I am deeply grateful to him and to Jean Marie Hiesberger, who helped me with some of the interviews. I thank Jean Marie also for her advice on the shaping of this book and for her editing of the manuscript.

I must acknowledge all of the people willing to be interviewed for this book and for those willing to contribute interesting stories about John Sullivan's life. Those who were willing to interrupt their busy schedules for lengthy interviews include Brother Emmett Berney, S.J., Father Norman Rotert, Father Richard Carney, Father William Bauman, Sister Jean Beste, BVM, Jean Marie Hiesberger, James Tierney, George Noonan, Neal Colby, Joseph Connor, Sister Judith Warmbold, DC, Father Patrick Rush, Joseph McGee, Betty Davies, Father James Jones, OSB, Father Gerald Waris, Father Mike Roach, Brother Michael Fehrenbach, FSC, Sister Vickie Perkins, SCL, Father John Schuele, Father Dennis Dorney, Rose Strothmann, Marvin Austin, Donna Murphy, Jim White, Mary Anne Slattery, Sister Barbara Austin, OSB, Mary Agnes Sullivan, Sister Cele Breen, SCL, Father James O'Kane, Maureen Kelly, Lou Falcon, Cardinal Bernard Law, Msgr. Joseph P. Herrard, Sister Perpetua McGrath, SCL, Sister Rosemary Ferguson, OP, Father Charles Torpey, Father Bernard Berger, Father Thomas Biller, Bishop John Leibrecht, Bishop George Fitzsimons, Archbishop Thomas Murphy, Bishop Ricardo Ramirez, Bishop William Friend, Bishop Walter Sullivan, Archbishop Peter Gerety, Bishop Charles Buswell, Sister Miriam Schnoebelen, OSB, Martha Fisch, Father James White, Sister Regina McCarthy, Patty Waltemath, Martha Conant, Mary Pat Storms, Father David Monahan and Karen Meyerott.

My sincere thanks to those persons who provided important research materials and information for the book, including Bishop Sullivan, Sister Martha Mary McGaw, CSJ, Father David Monahan, Sister Barbara Austin, OSB, Sister Miriam Schnoebelen, OSB, Donna Murphy, Theresa Carson (of the Catholic Church Extension Society), Father Marvin Leven, Jean Marie Hiesberger, Julie Asher (of Catholic News Service) and Father James White. Sister Joan Markley, SL, and Albert de Zutter helped by allowing me access to the archives of the Diocese of Kansas City-St. Joseph, Missouri, and *The Catholic Key* newspaper. Kathy Powers of the Diocese of Kansas City-St. Joseph helped with many long-distance details and Betty Betts, Karen Flynn and Carol Hogan helped with the proofreading of chapters.

Finally, I must thank James Tierney, Father Norman Rotert and Jean Marie Hiesberger, who wanted to pursue the idea of a book on Bishop John J. Sullivan, and those good friends of Bishop Sullivan whose financial assistance made this project possible, including Mr. and Mrs. Byron G. Thompson, Mrs. Rose Sarli Teicher, Mr. and Mrs. Joseph J. McGee, Jr., Mrs. Henry J. Massman III, Mr. and Mrs. James Flanagan, Mr. and Mrs. James P. Tierney, and Mr. and Mrs. Robert I. Donnellan. I am privileged that they asked me to write this biography. It is my contribution to honoring a man who has given his life to a consistent vision of the Gospel.

Preface

"IF A MAN OR WOMAN HAS A CHANCE, AN OPPORTUNITY TO HEAR the truth and rejects it, then I can live with that. But if a person never has a chance to hear, then I cannot sleep nights. You and I are sitting on the most earthshaking truths of all and have so much to say to the men and women of our time. Some of us may do it by preaching and a variety of pastoral ministries, but all of us *must do it* by the witness of our lives."

These words from Bishop John Joseph Sullivan's homily at his installation in 1977 as pastoral leader of the Diocese of Kansas City-St. Joseph, Missouri characterize the life of this priest and bishop. For 50 years he has been a living witness of the Catholic faith to the people he encountered in his ministry. His greatness and his simplicity are that he led others by his vision of faith. He made sure people had the opportunity to hear the simple truths of the Gospel.

Early in his priestly ministry, John Sullivan sensed his call to serve the church in this way and carried that focus throughout his years as a pastor and bishop. He had compassion for people, placed trust in them and initiated new efforts in trying to live out this vision. His constant inspiration was the "mission" territory of Oklahoma, where he first experienced the importance of shared ministry among priests, women religious and laypeople.

Nearly all of the people interviewed for this book were quick to describe John Sullivan as "a people person." "I don't think John Sullivan's ever met a stranger," says Cardinal Bernard Law of Boston. "He amazes you by who he knows and that he knows so much about you."

People and relationships are "the bottom line" for John, says Father Norman Rotert, a longtime friend who served as vicar general for the bishop in the Diocese of Kansas City-St. Joseph. "Knowing people and being known by people — that's a theme he has insisted on. He expected pastors to know people. That's because he modeled this on his own ability to know people, to know their names and all sorts of things about them. . . . This is a key factor in his whole ministry and theology. And I think this resulted in his emphasis on lay ministry and the priesthood of the faithful."

Perhaps it was John Sullivan's relationships with people — from the best theologians to the people in the pews — that helped him sense how to implement the spirit and content of the Second Vatican Council in his pastoral ministry. Vatican II gave an underpinning to his own instincts about where the church was headed in modern times. He took the thrust of *Lumen Gentium* (the Dogmatic Constitution on the Church) to heart — the inclusive, Scripture-based, communal model of the church as "the people of God." He did the same with the decree on the lay apostolate (*Apostolicam Actuositatem*), which urged the laity "to collaborate energetically in every apostolic and missionary undertaking sponsored by their local parish." Some say John Sullivan was almost prophetic in sensing that lay ministry needed to take a larger role in the American church in the 20th century.

He summarized his vision in part, on his 10th anniversary as bishop of Kansas City-St. Joseph, by writing, "A person becomes a Christian and a member of the church by baptism. That is a theological fact. A sociological fact is that most believers live out their faith and vocation as a Christian through parental and familial responsibilities, domestic duties and the demands of earning a living. They are witnesses within the fabric of daily existence. Yet there are others, fewer in number, who have responded to their faith by practicing special ministries in the church. This is a great gift to our church and one for which I am most grateful. . . . The laity are not correctly seen as an arm of the clergy with an episcopal mandate to reach the parts the clergy cannot reach. They are ordinary believers whose mandate is their baptism and who draw their energy from the Eucharist."

Many who know John identify two trademarks of his leadership as his ability to enable and inspire others to serve, and to put the Catholic faith in perspective to life's situations through the use of humor.

"His is a wonderful combination of commitment to people, to the church, to faith and to life," says Archbishop Thomas J. Murphy of Seattle. "There's something about John Sullivan that when you hear about Christian joy, you think of him. There's always that glint in his eye. The man has more stories on file than *Reader's Digest*. And the stories are always appropriate, tasteful, and speak to the situation at hand . . . Something about his whole demeanor and style puts people at ease."

Adds Bishop William B. Friend of Shreveport, Louisiana, "A true leader is one who initiates and enables others to action and does so in a manner that the people involved forget the source of their inspiration. John Sullivan has this gift . . . He took suggestions seriously. He had the gift of timing. He knew that if you want something you don't press continually, but you have the perseverance and patience to wait it out."

Certainly Bishop John Sullivan had the patience to wait for change as well as the will to effect change. As a bishop "I have certain responsibilities and must live with the decisions that are made," he said in 1990. "At the same time I am a product of my culture and can easily rely on old habits. The challenge to me and the challenge of the church is to get beyond comfortable habits and take risks that go contrary to the familiar."

Foreword

IN ALL OUR LIVES THERE ARE MOMENTS OF GRACE WHEN GOD'S
presence touches us in a profound way. Such grace often
comes unexpectedly in events, circumstances and experiences
which prompt us to stop and reflect on how God speaks to us.
At times, God's grace comes to us through the people who
enter our lives.

This biography of Bishop John J. Sullivan is a story of
grace. It is not only the account of the ministry of grace that
Bishop Sullivan offered to people as priest and bishop. It is
also the story of a man who was and is a grace to the
Church, to society, and especially to the people whose lives
he touched in remarkable ways.

For many of us, grace is a reality that belongs to the
supernatural order. It is a reality impossible to feel or touch,
hear or see. Yet, to meet Bishop John Sullivan is to experience God's grace. It is a grace that takes on human dimen-
sions in a towering man whose eyes and broad smile embrace
all who are present. It is a grace that comes alive in the immediate acceptance and respect he offers to each and every
person. It is a grace that speaks in the stories of human foi-
bles that he shares with a broad smile and the darting eyes
of a child who delights in the listening ears and faces of
those who are present. It is the grace of a man with a vision
and love of the Church and the ministry he offers as priest
and bishop.

To read this story, then, is to read a story of grace. More than anything else, it is a story of the grace of passion, a passion for people and the Kingdom of God. It is a passion shaped by fidelity to the mission and ministry of Jesus. To know Bishop John Sullivan is to experience God's grace.

There is an Irish fable of the King of Kerry who, upon dying, finds himself standing at heaven's entrance. However, he is unable to enter heaven because he wants to bring with him a piece of Kerry turf from his native land. He seeks the saints of heaven to intercede on his behalf, but to no avail. Even the Blessed Virgin Mary and Jesus Himself are unable to be of assistance. Reluctantly, he places the piece of Kerry turf on the ground to enter heaven unencumbered. He enters heaven with a heavy heart only to discover that he is back home in Kerry.

When God calls Bishop John Sullivan home, I believe John would like to bring his dreams and hopes with him. Like most of us, he will be disappointed to be told to leave them behind and to just bring himself. Yet, I believe that when John meets our good and gracious God in eternity, he could well find himself back in his Oklahoma parishes, his Extension office, the local churches of Grand Island and Kansas City, with all his dreams that have become a reality.

Bishop John J. Sullivan has been and is a grace to me as person, Christian, priest and bishop. I give thanks for the grace that God has given me and countless others in the life and ministry of this holy man.

Thomas J. Murphy
Archbishop of Seattle
October 20, 1994

CHAPTER ONE

The Formative Years

TO LISTEN TO JOHN JOSEPH SULLIVAN RECOUNT HIS YEARS AS A youngster in Kansas and Oklahoma, one immediately senses how deeply a dual influence — that of his parents and a certain pioneer Catholic spirit — was scripted into the text of his life. It was an influence he carried with him as seminarian, priest and bishop.

His parents were American born, but ancestors on both sides were irreversibly Irish. His mother, Mary Berney Sullivan, had roots in Wicklow and Carlow counties in Ireland. His father, Walter Sullivan, had family roots in County Kerry. Walter and Mary were married in St. Joseph's Church in Everest, Kansas.

John was born on July 5, 1920, in Horton, Kansas, 27 miles west of Atchison, and lived there until he was 10 years old. The family then moved to Edmond, Oklahoma, on the outskirts of Oklahoma City. The family of five — Walter, Mary, his grandmother on his mother's side, John and his younger brother Dan — had a strong faith. "I was fortunate to be in a family that had your typical troubles, but you really felt, you understood in a limited way what Christ meant when he said 'Love one another as I have loved you,'" John recalls. "And no one loved us like our parents loved us. . . . It was a relationship in which you never felt exploited. It wasn't a question of give-and-take, but it was give and give and give. They didn't expect anything in return."

John credits his mother — a strikingly handsome, sensitive woman — for instilling in him a vocation to service, "what today we call justice and peace, but with the faith dimension being very prominent and important," he says. Her faith had a quiet, unpretentious depth — her religious beliefs were not confined to Sunday but were a part of her daily existence. While growing up during the Depression years of the 1930s, he recalls, "Mother had a lot of compassion for the poor — a concern for people, their physical welfare as well as their spiritual."

When John was about 13, his parents bought an old farm west of Marlow. His father, whom he describes as a "mechanical genius," was working for the Electro-Motive Company, a railroad subsidiary of General Motors, servicing the locomotives. The farm was rented out to a poor family. "It was an awful place — peanuts, cotton and poverty," John recalls. "We would go down occasionally to try to fix it up. My mother thought this was a good idea. That really left an impression on me. She always had the art of thinking up good ideas and rallying us to her cause. We were poor, but that family was really poor. . . . When I was at St. Benedict's College and considering the priesthood, I often thought of that family. They were poor in money with no resources to draw on, they were culturally poor, and they were spiritually poor, it seemed. As I thought of them, I realized that people counted, that they were a big priority in my life. It made me want to help people."

During those years Walter Sullivan, "a feisty little Irishman," traveled extensively for his work. It fell to Mary to take care of the family. John attended John Carroll grade school and high school at Our Lady's Cathedral parish, where he served as an altar boy for Bishop Francis Clement Kelley. John was extremely close to his brother, Dan, who was six years younger. "Mother was so fond of Dan," John says. "As he got older, Dan responded to all the opportunities he had as far as witnessing to the faith. His whole interest was in helping the poor."

Challenges in Oklahoma

The struggles of the small Catholic population (about 3%) in Oklahoma during the 1930s had as great an impact on John's young life as his parents. "Catholics couldn't drift — you had to swim upstream," he remembers. "You had to struggle to persevere. I saw people suffering, and the response of the people around me was one of support and heroic assistance."

When John returned later as a priest, "I called on one old Irishman. He told me he hadn't seen a priest for 55 years. 'Where have you been?' he asked me. 'I didn't leave the church. The church left me.'" There was "so much anti-Catholic feeling in the state that I saw that as a very worthy challenge," John recalls. "The challenge was to reach out to people and to be concerned about their quality of life. We knew in Oklahoma there was no such thing as a lone ranger."

Bishop Kelley was a man of imagination and great ability who founded the Catholic Church Extension Society and made it into the most successful home missions society in U.S. Catholic history. He served from 1924 to 1944 in the Diocese of Oklahoma (the diocese was renamed the Diocese of Oklahoma City and Tulsa on Nov. 24, 1930), emphasizing a far-flung evangelization program in the 70,000-square-mile diocese. Among his innovative missionary efforts in Oklahoma were door-to-door census takings, the construction of regional mission houses to serve rural areas, and many public speeches. But with a suddenness that must have been shattering, Bishop Kelley found his diocese and himself impoverished by the Great Depression. The church was mired in debt and so restricted financially that only the most minimal services could be provided.

One of Bishop Kelley's primary goals was establishing better relations between the Catholic community and the Oklahoma public, including other church communions. "He did so much to correct prejudice and bigotry," John Sullivan recalls. "He taught all of us religious tolerance. . . . He was a scholar and a prolific writer." Involvement of the laity was a key factor in the evangelical and instruction work, although Bishop Kelley was admittedly frustrated by the consistent drift of parishioners from the rural areas into the cities or out of the state. He saw his state as a missionary field where every resource should be aimed at making converts and reconciling fallen-away Catholics.

When Bishop Kelley came to Oklahoma, there were 75 diocesan priests. European-born priests — particularly the Belgians and the Dutch — were still the dominant group. There were only a few native Oklahomans. From the year Bishop Kelley took office to near the end of his active ministry, Oklahoma's diocesan priests increased by one-third. Among the younger priests were a number of native sons who would serve as a source of vitality in the Oklahoma clergy for the next three decades.

"Catholics and the clergy in Oklahoma were generally more open to possible innovations in church ministry because they historically constituted such a tiny minority in a Bible-belt state known for its anti-Catholic attitudes," says Father James White, historian for the Diocese of Tulsa. "For example, John Sullivan's predecessor as pastor of The Madalene in Tulsa was Irish-born James McNamee. He was ordained in 1925, and 10 years later shocked American Catholics nationwide with an article proposing the use of English in the liturgy, at least in mission areas. (Kelley knew of the article's publication beforehand and supported Father McNamee in the ensuing controversy.)"

Choosing the priesthood

It was against this background that John Sullivan chose the priesthood. His decision was partially influenced by a feeling of emptiness amid adolescent fun. Young John was a handsome and active teenager. He loved to dance and drive motor cars and played basketball at John Carroll High

School. Early in his high school years, he had some serious thoughts about what to pursue in his life.

There was a basketball game one evening, followed by a dance. Afterward, he recalls, "I drove into the garage and just sat there thinking. The game and the dance were fun, but what did it all mean? This wasn't it." During his senior year, he started cutting through the Cathedral grounds on his way home for lunch. Then he began stopping in to pray.

One night, as he often did in the summer, John took to the front porch of the house to sleep on a cot to help escape the intense heat. His mother, in a rocking chair, was saying the rosary. John told his mother in a half-whisper that he wanted to become a priest. There was no answer for quite some time. Then Mary Sullivan said, "Well, that's good," he recalls. "But if you ever want to come out of the seminary, we'll be on the front porch to greet you."

Walter Sullivan thought John at age 16 was too young to enter the seminary. He suggested John go to St. Benedict's College in Atchison, Kansas, for two years, looking to make sure that his son had a true vocation. "I'd had four years of Latin at John Carroll. My dad said if I still wanted to be a priest after the two years, I could go to the seminary. And he kept his word," John recalls. When he entered Kenrick Seminary in St. Louis in 1939, he joined a class of 47 seminarians. "We went through in a hurry," he says of his war-time studies for the priesthood. "I felt that once I decided to become a priest, I chose to go home to Oklahoma because the people were poor and they didn't have much opportunity or exposure to their faith, because Catholics were so few in number. I thought that was kind of important. I was interested in their physical and spiritual well-being and their quality of life."

John was ordained for the Diocese of Oklahoma City and Tulsa on September 23, 1944 at age 24 by Bishop Albert Fletcher of Little Rock, Arkansas, because Bishop Kelley was in poor health. Three others were ordained with him in Our Lady's Cathedral in Oklahoma City: Fathers Bill Swift, Bernard Havlik and Francis Warnke. Rookie priests John Sullivan and Bill Swift celebrated their first Masses within days of each other, continuing a friendship that had begun while they were classmates at St. Benedict's College.

Over the years John Sullivan has never regretted his decision to become a priest. "Being a priest — with the ambitions I had about commitment to people, with the opportunity to be united to the Lord, to celebrate the Eucharist — was what I intended 100%, with my whole heart and whole soul. With that commitment, you could put everything else aside."

CHAPTER TWO

Early Pastoral Experiences

JOHN SULLIVAN'S EARLY YEARS AS A PRIEST WERE DURING A time of building and development of a truly native Oklahoma clergy under the energetic Bishop Eugene McGuinness. First and foremost with Bishop McGuiness was the extension of the church.

Bishop Kelley had suffered a heart attack in October 1942, and struggled through five years of illness before his death on Feb. 1, 1948. He had brought a mood of excitement and vitality to the church in Oklahoma, but lived to see many of his plans frustrated or fail. Bishop McGuinness, who had worked for 18 years with the Catholic Church Extension Society, inspired lay people, religious and clergy during his tenure from 1945 to 1957, John recalls. "He embodied his motto, 'All things to all people.' He loved the church and had a vision of where we were headed."

Shortly after his ordination, John was named assistant pastor at Holy Family Cathedral in Tulsa. He served as director of Catholic Activities — an organization for single adults 18 and older that involved some 1,500 people — and acted as Catholic chaplain at the University of Tulsa. His best friend, Bill Swift, served at a neighboring parish. Father David Monahan, now a priest in Oklahoma City, was then a senior in high school thinking of entering the priesthood. He knew both priests. "Everyone in Tulsa knew everyone else. John was the handsome young priest that had all the girls swooning at him," he recalls. "Right away it was obvious he was a person with lots of zeal and dynamism and he had an appeal to people. He seemed so fervent about what he was doing. I don't think he's ever lost that."

Youth movement

During these years after World War II, a series of study conferences and youth rallies brought the Young Christian Student (YCS) movement to life in Oklahoma under the inspiration of Father Donald Kanaly, who had studied in Belgium under Canon Joseph Cardijn. The youth rallies of the late 1940s and early 1950s featured parades, pageants and colorful outdoor celebrations of the Eucharist. In this context, John Sullivan and Bill Swift gave passionate, funny and challenging talks to youngsters on being a Catholic in Oklahoma.

Benedictine Sister Miriam Schnoebelen was a high school student from Northwest rural Oklahoma when she first met John at a statewide youth conference hosted by the Benedictines on their Monte Cassino campus in Tulsa. "I was one of the few in the crowd who went directly to them (Sullivan and Swift) after they shared the podium," she recalls. "I wanted to find out if they *really* knew — from their own experience as teenagers — what it was like to live in a place where the only Catholics were your relatives; where a Bible-belt mentality pervaded and controlled all activities in the town; where going to movies and playing cards were 'sins'; where dancing, well that certainly was the work of the devil; and where Catholics were off-limits as friends.

"I've often wondered if that first encounter with Jack (John) was the reason he 'kept track' of me," Sister Miriam adds. "I was quite unaware that he had done so until I went to college in Guthrie. It was there I discovered he had remembered me. More than that, he had taken the time to find out more about me than I would have revealed had I been the source of this information. Lots of knowledge was factual but some was intuitive which, in a sense, was both awesome and scary to this 18-year-old."

At first Bishop McGuinness had other plans for John Sullivan than his assignment in Tulsa. Early in the summer of 1945, while on a priests' retreat, the bishop approached John. "We were very short on priests at the time," John recalls. "I passed Bishop McGuinness on the driveway. He said 'I want to see you in my room in 20 minutes.' So I went to his room and he told me he was going to send me to the Catholic University of America to study canon law. And that I couldn't tell anyone but my parents. Even at that early date I was disappointed — that was not really what I wanted to do. But I was ready to go.

"Bishop McGuinness said some priests were being loaned to Oklahoma by an Eastern diocese and I wouldn't be gone long. So I prepared myself attitudinally. Then in August I got a phone call from him saying these priests couldn't come. So the bishop put it off until the next year. So I had this study assignment pending all the time — it was a real distraction."

In the summer of 1947, John was enrolled at the Catholic University of America. Before he left Oklahoma, the pastor of St. Mary's Church in Guthrie died. "I was going to Guthrie to be master of ceremonies at the funeral. Bishop McGuinness called and told me to come by his house first. He said he was going to station me in Guthrie for one year. So he drove up there with me that afternoon. And I ended up being there 12 years," John says.

Zealous young pastor

John became pastor of St. Mary's in Guthrie, some 30 miles north of Oklahoma City, in July 1947. His keen ability to reach out to people, to remember their names, and to show concern for each of them made him unique as a pastor in the often hostile environment of this Mason-dominated town of some 12,000 people. His zeal made a big impact, both on Catholics and non-Catholics.

At the urging of Bishop McGuinness, and with a substantial donation he arranged, John helped to reopen St. Mary's School in 1948. It had been closed in 1933 during the Great Depression. The Benedictine sisters considered St. Mary's the "miracle school." It seemed impossible that a parish with only 125 families that had been without a Catholic school for 15 years could in seven months erect a $70,000 modern, well-equipped school. The original St. Mary's had been the first school the Benedictines had opened in Oklahoma Territory in 1889, only five months after the historical land run which opened the territory to white settlers. When the new school opened on Sept. 7, 1948, it boasted almost 100% enrollment, with 109 students (25 in kindergarten). John Sullivan taught religion in all the classes.

Sister Miriam taught at St. Mary's. "My Benedictine community already had a history of providing educational opportunities — though separate — for the black people in Guthrie," she notes. "Before it was the political thing to do, we began integration at St. Mary's. Jack's attitude was 'It's the right thing to do . . . so let's do it!' He made no big fuss as he paved the way with the people in the parish. As we buffered insensitive remarks from both the faith and the civic communities, he stood with us through the transition.

"Jack was a promise-keeper. He would not let anyone down when he could see even the slightest possible solution to their need. For example, when people from outlying communities wanted to send their children to St. Mary's, we got a bus. He added to his list of doing with and for the people by driving the bus himself."

A tremendous influence

Catholic institutional life was at its zenith in Guthrie at this time. The Benedictine sisters' motherhouse, college, boarding school and hospital were all flourishing. The legendary Dominican Father George Carpentier, a close friend and strong influence on John, was busy all over Logan County. Father Carpentier, pastor of St. Catherine's, the black parish in Guthrie, "gave me such a sense of ultimate reality," John says. "Carp had a tremendous influence on me as far as priorities were concerned: people and compassion for the poor, immediate and long-term. His prayer life was an example to me."

John and Father Carpentier would together visit the Catholic families in the small town of Crescent. "When Carp went to visit his people, he'd bring them cans of corn and tomatoes wrapped in *Our Sunday Visitor*," John recalls. "He was such a character, out on the roads visiting his people to find out if they had enough to eat and how he could help them. They loved him."

John calls his years in Guthrie — his longest time as a pastor anywhere — "one of the most exciting periods of my life. I just cared very much for all the people. I wanted to improve their quality of life. We had tremendous poverty. Some of the farms southeast of town wouldn't bring more than $4 or $5 an acre. About 25% of the county was black.

"I realized I could minister most to the families by caring for them and especially for the kids," John says. "There were many tragedies and I tried to be there. At various times there would be great opportunities to help. The priority for me was to be with the people, whether they were Catholic or not. We had Masons received into the Church and their wives didn't even know it. Some of us got to be pretty good friends." John often visited patients in Benedictine Heights Hospital. "I saw one beautiful girl with asthma. I started going out to see the family," he recalls. "I would go every Sunday night and have ice cream and sit under a tree. They liked that. And the girls — Mildred was graduating and Doris was one year behind her. All six members of the family eventually became members of St. Mary's. . . . And we got Mildred and Doris eventually to graduate from St. Mary's College in Leavenworth, Kansas."

John influenced many people's lives. "During my initial formation years as a Benedictine, Jack kept me real true to myself," Sister Miriam remembers. "He encouraged my passion for justice while gently holding me back — with good timing — when I tended to 'make things right' with what could have been imprudent boldness. . . . When I was introduced to discernment as a way of life for a Benedictine, I knew Jack was the one who enabled me, as an adult, to approach life responses in a reflective, discerning way."

Sister Miriam recalls Guthrie as a Masonic stronghold. "At the south end of town sat a Masonic Consistory — purported to be, at that time, the largest in the world. On the opposite horizon, the Benedictine monastery for women and their high school-college stood tall. In between the two, the steeple of St. Mary's Church and Benedictine Heights Hospital dominated the skyline. I felt there was a profound, respectful and healthy cooperation between the Benedictine community and Jack Sullivan."

An alluring group of people

She adds, "The Catholic community in Guthrie mystified me. They were not like any other people I'd experienced . . . perhaps I can say they were a disparate but alluring group of people. I perceived this to be, at least somewhat, the result of their living in the shadow of a Masonic powerbase, combined with rampant stories about Catholics, priests and nuns. They seemed frozen and cowed which, for many, resulted in not even daring to let others know they were Catholic. This certainly kept some from church services. The prejudice toward Catholics was so real there had been some blatant public activities of the Ku Klux Klan directed at their pastor just a few years before Jack was assigned there. This was the scene Jack immersed himself in as a young pastor. . . . The Catholic community came into its own when John was their pastor. Under his leadership they grew in wisdom and grace, proud to be identified as Catholic."

Martha Fisch, who still lives in Guthrie, was a young married woman at the time John Sullivan became pastor. He baptized her four children. "He was a green parish priest, delightful and handsome, very humble, and he just won everyone's heart," she recalls. "He made quite an impact on this town, which was and is still predominantly Masonic. He was well-liked by everyone, and that's unusual. He built the school and staffed it with young, energetic nuns. He could talk you out of your eyeballs. He had a way about him, and we worked like Trojans for him. He was very gregarious. He was always wanting to put on a dinner, and we probably had more of them than any parish in Oklahoma."

For Martha, John was often a lifesaver in times when she was downhearted or troubled. "He had such tremendous faith that everything would be all right, and he could always convince me of that," she says. "He was a big cigar smoker, and in those days we didn't lock our homes. One day I was upstairs scrubbing the bathtub and I smelled a cigar. I knew he'd come in the back door. I was crying because there wasn't enough money for my daughter's tuition at St. Mary's College. I'd thrown a bar of soap into the hallway. I told him what was wrong, and he assured me it would all work out. I said 'God doesn't write checks.' He told me I was mistaken."

Marvin Austin, now 80, helped John raise money for St. Mary's school and parish. "We lived just one block from the church, and he was always at our house," Austin says. "We were together a lot trying to raise funds. We went to see this man with a couple of oil wells on his place eight miles west of town. Sullivan says, 'We're going to get $5,000 from him.' But we talked to him for quite a while and came back empty-handed. And we cried all the way home."

John "could get almost anyone to do anything," Austin adds. "My dad had eight kids and he had never joined the Church. He was a 32nd-degree Mason. But before Father Sullivan left, my dad was a Catholic. He really had that kind of impact on people."

John went into one household where he discovered a young man, physically disabled from birth, who had been confined to his home most of his life. "This young man, in his 20s, was bright, intelligent, witty and joyful," Sister Miriam recalls. "No one outside the family had gotten to share this gift of personhood until Jack introduced him to our world at the church. A first outing was to Christmas midnight Mass. He sat — all folded up in a little red wagon right in the doorway which opened into the sanctuary. I'll never forget the ecstatic look on his face as he participated in the celebration. Jack was the one who had seen to it that he got there by going himself to the home and making all the preparations and bringing him to the church.

"Many times after that — at least weekly — Jack would go into the home to get him out of bed, dress him, fix his breakfast, share stories and the latest sports statistics, and always pray with him and bring Communion. . . . Jack showed tenderness and compassion with people. He totally involved himself with the person he was serving."

Lay ministry in practice

With the great distances that St. Mary's embraced, with the few Catholics that were present, and with the great need for evangelization, John came to realize that he could not do everything needed by himself, according to his friend, Father Bill Swift.

"Jack literally went into the community and outlying areas to find Catholics," Sister Miriam confirms. "In this ministry he encouraged the gift of a particular woman who did outreach to fallen-away Catholics. Her volunteer work was recognized as an important, vital extension of the role of the pastor. I would say this was collaborative lay ministry in practice before it was a byword in the post-Vatican II era."

The woman was Rose Strothmann, now 89 and living in Oklahoma City. As a single woman when John was pastor, she lived with her mother on the family farm at Mulhall, about 14 miles from Guthrie. After her mother's death in September 1948, John told her of his plans to build a mission church in Mulhall and asked for her help. "The church had been closed in 1907 and many Catholics fell away," John recalls. "In fact, one farmer showed me the rafters in his house that had come out of the old church. We worked to build a new little church for about $4,000."

Rose, a certified teacher, systematically set out to canvas the entire county (including Mulhall and Crescent), meeting with people to talk with them about their personal faith, and to learn of community needs. "Even though she knew many of the people, the reception she got was really something," John says. "I'd follow her, sometimes during the day and sometimes in the evening. . . . Sometimes, after weeks of preparation you would go out and there would be no one there for the inquiry class. So the next day I'd go to the barber shop and the hardware store to try and get people. I kept thinking this isn't going to work. But we were persistent and it did."

The hope for renewed community

Rose's work began almost exclusively as a mission to alienated and unchurched Catholics. In its purest form, "what she brought to those she visited was the offer of friendship and the hope for renewed community," John says. "She was unafraid to share with people her understanding of the good news, nor was she reluctant to question people about their values, hopes and concerns. I think she offered them support. I know she offered them sincere affection."

Rose remembers fondly how she and John worked together in religious instruction classes in Mulhall before the church was built in 1953. "It was really amazing because many people had a background as Catholics, but hadn't been able to practice their faith because they were too far from a church. One year we had 26 people from Mulhall, the largest class ever, baptized in St. Mary's Church. And Father Sullivan wanted me to get the school annual so that he could learn everyone's name." Adds John, "Without the benefit of a church building, we still had a thriving, dynamic catechumenate. It was Rose who prepared these people for baptism, and it was on account of her willingness to serve as an agent of the Spirit, of her willingness to minister, that our community grew."

Later, after her brother married, Rose moved off the farm and into Guthrie in a small apartment across the street from St. Mary's. She started a similar door-to-door census of Logan County, and also worked at Benedictine Heights Hospital with mentally retarded children. "I was almost 50 years old when taking the census," Rose says. "At the time all I could think about was I was spreading the word of the Catholic religion. I didn't think too much about the fact that I was a lay woman doing this. All I knew was that Father Sullivan wanted me to do it and he encouraged me, so I did it." Recalls John, "I might have had more confidence in lay people like Rose than some other priests did. But I felt that unless you give people a wide berth, even though they might make mistakes, you'll never know what they can do. If you're going to inhibit or restrict them, it just won't work."

New and creative ways

Rose and John worked together in ministry for 11 years. When she left to teach at St. Patrick's School in Oklahoma City and he left to be pastor of St. James Parish there in 1959, St. Mary's in Guthrie had grown to some 220 families. In later years, John would look back on this shared ministry and recognize how his personal experience taught him the importance of lay ministry more than theological reflection or dialogue. "In 1948, the role of the laity as formal, 'professional' representatives of the church might be discussed as a remote possibility but never conceived as an acceptable practice," John wrote in 1983.

"Looking back, I am grateful that I was ordained for a mission diocese. When you don't have the resources — either financial or people resources — you are forced to use what you have in new and often creative ways. I never questioned the appropriateness of Rose ministering to people — to officially represent the Catholic church and our parish to others. I never entertained doubts concerning the confusion of lay and clerical roles, nor did I feel threatened as a pastor that someone else was doing (and possibly doing better) the work which at the time was regarded as the work of the priest, or in some acceptable instances, the work of non-ordained religious.

"I saw in Rose the benefits of outstanding lay ministry on two levels," John added. "First, it was obvious her work was yielding real, identifiable fruit. She was touching people's lives, she was evangelizing, she was enriching and enlarging the body of Christ. Second, I saw in her another dynamic: the more she ministered, the more she developed in her ministry skills, the more frequently she was called upon to represent Christ in this world, the more her personal faith grew. The thought that personal faith and personal ministry are inseparable is hardly a novel idea. However, seeing this dynamic operative in Rose made me keenly aware of how easy it is for those of us in pastoral leadership to challenge persons to grow in faith without providing them assistance in developing that faith into ministry."

The decade of the 1950s proved to be a time of building not only for John Sullivan at St. Mary's in Guthrie, but for the entire church in Oklahoma. During Bishop McGuinness' 13-year tenure in Oklahoma City and Tulsa, the number of Catholics in the state grew by almost 40% to more than 93,000 in 1957. In the last year of his life, 1,242 adult converts were received into the Church. Religious vocations also flourished. "When Bishop McGuinness spoke, he emphasized the greatness of Oklahoma Catholics and the need for a native-born clergy," John remembers. "In 1953, he ordained 15 Oklahomans to the priesthood. In 1958, when I went to Rome with two other priests, our diocese had more students at the North American College than any other diocese except the Archdiocese of New York."

To those who knew him, John Sullivan typified what Bishop McGuinness liked in his priests: energetic, action-oriented and willing to work himself bone-weary on behalf of the Church. "In those days you saw him in rolled-up shirt sleeves with a cigar in his mouth as often as not," says Sister Mary Helen McInerney, a member of the Sisters of Charity of Leavenworth, who knew John in Guthrie, and later worked with him in Oklahoma City and Kansas City. "He was a loved man who had a special way of relating to people. He had a way of influencing young people so that they would want to go out and set the world on fire. . . . As a young priest he took people's problems to heart."

CHAPTER THREE

The Extension Years: The Larger Mission Church

THE END OF 1957 SAW THE DEATH OF BISHOP MCGUINNESS before he could ordain his newly named auxiliary, Monsignor Victor J. Reed, then rector of Tulsa's Holy Family Cathedral. As a result, Victor Reed became bishop of Oklahoma City and Tulsa on March 5, 1958.

Soon after, Bishop Reed appointed a committee of John Sullivan, Msgr. Gavan Monaghan, Msgr. Sylvester Luecke and Msgr. Charles Buswell to design a program called "Oklahoma volunteers." The concept was that Catholic colleges would be profitable places to seek young Catholic volunteers for missionary areas of Oklahoma. Bishop Reed thought the volunteers could help ensure that Catholics had the opportunity for quality religious education, John recalls. "He was concerned about the dwindling enrollment of the Catholic schools and the ability of all the people in the diocese to be knowledgeable about their faith."

That summer, Bishop Reed sent John, Father Bill Swift and Bill Nerin (in place of Bishop McGuinness) to lead a pilgrimage to Europe as part of the 100th anniversary of the apparition of Our Lady of Lourdes. "It was during this pilgrimage that I experienced an event which would shape my belief in the importance of ministry for all believers and the intrinsic value of lay ministry," John says.

In Sorrento, he met a group of students from Trinity College in Washington, D.C. "For these women, the slums of Naples were their first contact with the extreme poverty of post-World War II Europe," he says. "What I found interesting in hearing their reactions was their ability to assess what they had seen from the perspective of the believer. Having witnessed poverty, they could not easily dismiss it without some form of response, without some gesture of mercy. They wanted to do something and they were frustrated by their inability to act. I pondered their questions. They had youth and energy and faith. And I had seen terrible poverty right in Oklahoma. These young women could help the poor without ever leaving their own country. So a few years before the Peace Corps, I was witnessing an energy of spirit which needed to be tapped."

Shortly after returning to Oklahoma, John wrote to three colleges in the New York City area — New Rochelle, Mount St. Vincent's and Manhattanville — as well as Trinity College, inviting students to come to Oklahoma to experience work in a mission diocese. That autumn, he went to those colleges to plead his case. As a result, 50 students came to Oklahoma in the summer of 1959, and 15 others came for the entire year. By May 1959, John had left St. Mary's in Guthrie to become pastor of St. James Parish in Oklahoma City.

After his experience with lay ministry in Guthrie, "the idea of volunteers to help poor areas was very much on John's mind," says Bishop Charles Buswell, who before being named bishop of Pueblo, Colo., in 1959, was pastor of Christ the King Parish in Oklahoma City. "He truly believed the volunteers could be of assistance to the people in mission parishes that couldn't afford staff. The volunteers gave these people an understanding that they were the Church and not second-class citizens."

A *variety of ministries*

The young people were engaged in a variety of ministries touching people's lives or addressing the real needs of education, health care and spiritual consolation, John remembers. "While I do not minimize the benefits of their work, I could see the greatest good accomplished by these volunteers was what the experience of ministry did for themselves — how often it enriched their own faith lives and their values," he wrote in 1983. "Something basic happened during the process of service: the word of God ceased to be an abstraction for many of them, but became something real, rooted in the activities of their lives. By giving themselves to others in the name of our Lord, by their willingness to sacrifice, they learned to love God more deeply."

Sister Perpetua McGrath, a member of the Sisters of Charity of Leavenworth and principal of St. James School, recalls several of the volunteers serving as lay teachers. John wanted every child in the parish to be enrolled in the school, regardless of whether or not their family could pay. "He would go out and beat the bushes to find the children," she says. "I taught religious education on Sunday, and we only had one family with three children in the parish who were not in the school." The volunteers, she adds, "immediately knew that they could go to John if they were anxious or troubled. There wasn't a selfish bone in his body. It could be the middle of the night, and for anyone who needed him he was right there. . . . He converted many people by being so concerned about their well-being."

While the Oklahoma volunteers were in the beginning stages, Pope John XXIII encouraged the Church in North America (U.S. and Canada) to "tithe" 10% with their resources of dedicated people and money to the church in Latin America. Maryknoll Father John J. Considine was handed the task of initiating the extensive work of organizing the Papal Volunteers for Latin America (PAVLA). Father Considine thought that laypersons ought to be involved. At the same time, it was decided to have a home missions compo-

nent of volunteers, and for this Father Considine turned to
the Catholic Church Extension Society. The Extension Lay
Volunteers were born on paper in November 1960, according
to John. "Father Considine was a real operator. He asked
Cardinal Albert Meyer of Chicago (chancellor of the Extension Society) and Cardinal Richard Cushing of Boston (episcopal moderator of the Latin American bureau) for sister volunteer programs and they said yes. Then Meyer and Cushing asked every bishop in the country to appoint a diocesan
director and each Catholic college to appoint a faculty member liaison for the Extension Volunteers."

The original idea was that the Extension Volunteers
would be mostly a referral service for lay volunteers to home
mission dioceses. But the idea didn't fly, John recalls. To
make necessary changes, Msgr. John May (later the Bishop
of Mobile, Alabama, and the Archbishop of St. Louis, Missouri), general secretary of Extension, came to Oklahoma because he had heard of the Oklahoma volunteers. He bought
the concept and immediately drew the proven resources of
Oklahoma into the implementation of the Extension Volunteers. May asked Bishop Reed to assign John full time to
Extension to head the volunteer program. "John's work with
Extension was a direct result of his experience in the parishes of Oklahoma," says his friend, Father Bill Swift. "It
simply confirmed what he already knew and encouraged him
to find more and new ways to cope with the great need for
evangelization."

Moved across the country

John saw the Extension Volunteers effort divided into
three steps: recruitment/selection, orientation and in-service
support. For the next seven years (June 1961 to June 1968),
John moved across the country spreading the news of the volunteers. He visited most of the Catholic colleges in the nation. He also spoke at many Newman Centers on secular
campuses. Single persons and married couples between the

ages of 21 and 45 were asked to give at least one year of full-time service to the church.

The first orientation sessions featured many Oklahoma priests — among them Fathers Dan Allen, Joe Dillon, Bill Skeehan, Charles Swett, Philip Donohoe and Philip Wilkiemeyer. Several of the original Oklahoma volunteers helped — Connie (Scott) Kelly, Elizabeth McMahon (Jeep) and Mary Christie. Msgr. Luecke was named the national field director of the entire program (later succeeded by Father Thomas J. McCabe of the Boston Archdiocese). Father Wilkiemeyer became Oklahoma diocesan director of the Extension Volunteers. "Our biggest problem was to discover good ways in which these young people could help and to ease them into the work," John says. "We tried to deal with the problems of loneliness and motivation. Many of the volunteers were 21, and some were the first out of their families to get a college education. They had great expectations, and sometimes their parents' expectations were not the same as their own. These students were just generous and real idealists. Volunteering was a totally different experience for them."

During the seven years John directed the Extension Volunteers, some 1,500 Catholic volunteers participated. In one year, he recalls, there were 430 Extension Volunteers in 30 dioceses from Puerto Rico to Alaska. "It was an amazing outpouring of generosity," he notes. *The Oklahoma Courier's* Sept. 8, 1961 issue reported that 57 lay volunteers from 20 states had been assigned to Oklahoma. "Until next June they'll be at the mercy of Oklahoma's weather, roads and mission needs," the story read. *The Courier* reported the volunteers would be teaching school, serving as nurses, working in Newman Clubs and catechizing in parishes. The newspaper stated Extension Volunteers were also assigned to the Archdiocese of San Antonio and the Diocese of Amarillo. Commenting on the volunteers' reactions to Oklahoma, *The Courier* reporter noted, "So far they've found roads 'unbelievable,' dogs hostile and people warm and receptive."

Close friendship

John's work with Extension marked the beginning of a close friendship with John May, which would last more than three decades. May, a priest of the Archdiocese of Chicago, in 1959 was named general secretary and vice president of the Extension Society. He later served as president from 1967 to 1970. "We had a unique relationship," John says. "We were so close, yet we always argued some. In staff meetings we would try to persuade each other. One afternoon we really got into it. He said we should put priority on issues. I said our priority should be persons. Later we went to dinner with volunteer Jerry Ernst. Jerry walked by a kid on the sidewalk, patted his head, and said 'Hello, you little issue.' We all had to laugh."

Some prominent bishops of the 1960s also helped to shape John's vision of the changing Church and an increasing role for laypeople. He calls Cardinal Meyer (archbishop of Chicago from 1958 to 1965) one of his heroes. "One of his favorite expressions was from St. Paul, 'Don't stifle the spirit,'" says John. "I carried that idea with me when I assessed the whole question of personnel in the Church." He admires Cardinal John Dearden of Detroit (archbishop from 1958-80) for trying to bring Vatican II insights to bear on the American church. "He took up the cause of renewal," John recalls. "He undertook a diocesan synod in which thousands of people participated, both clergy and lay. It was a model for other dioceses."

Though he downplays his own part, John, as director of the Extension Volunteers, was a key figure, especially in the recruitment of volunteers. "His Irish charm, zeal and knowledge of home missions proved magnetic," wrote Sister Martha Mary McGaw, a member of the Sisters of St. Joseph of Carondelet, in a Jan. 20, 1980 article in *The Sooner Catholic* about the volunteers. "He was able to share happiness and grief. He laughed and cried with ease. He was human. He could understand. He could recruit."

Of all his engaging qualities, perhaps John's ability to remember people and their names had the most impact, says Donna Murphy, an Extension volunteer from 1963-66 and John's secretary in the Chicago office in 1967-68. "Once he had met someone, he would remember them. At our formal orientation for new volunteers in September 1963, it amazed me that at the end of the training he could go around the room and say our names, our hometowns, and what colleges we had attended. This really made a difference to the volunteers. Each person felt they were essential to the work."

Kathy Fox-Larsen, an Extension volunteer from 1967-69, first met John in the dining room at the University of Chicago where all the volunteers assembled for six weeks of training in the summer of 1967. "He was going from table to table greeting people and, much to my astonishment, he called me by name," she says. "He knew us because he studied our pictures from our applications."

A new sense of Church

John saw the volunteers as carrying out the mandates of Vatican II regarding the role of the laity. "His idea was what we all came to know at Vatican II — that the church is to be found in the people," assesses Bishop Buswell. "Volunteers got a totally new sense of church — they knew their role was as important as anybody else's." Msgr. Joseph Herrard of the Archdiocese of Dubuque, Iowa, who worked with John as training director of the volunteers from 1966-67, adds: "His vision was to see everyone brought to their personal fulfillment as Christians. He believed this came about because of their baptism. He had the insight and foresight to see this. He captured this idea even before Vatican II came along."

In a November 1966 paper titled "A New Concept of the Volunteer," John, noting that he had worked with more than 1,200 volunteers since 1961, suggested that lay volunteers no longer be called "home missioners." Men and women should be engaged in an internship for the adult apostolic Christian life. They would work not only in mission areas, but in urban and suburban areas. "We are convinced from our own observations and from discussions with a number of leading educators and specialists in pastoral work that a Catholic education is not really complete on graduation day," he wrote. "We believe that all Catholic young men and women should have a period of apostolic work directly for the church. The lay volunteer would be, then, not the rare person who volunteers for one or more years of mission service, but ordinary young Catholics, well-informed and dedicated, giving a year or more of service. . . . We believe that Vatican II teachings on the people of God, the laity, the universal call to perfection and the missionary nature of the church make it almost essential that as many young Catholics as possible have an opportunity for direct service to the church. We believe that the more this idea becomes prevalent, the more young Catholics will really understand their Christian identity and the mission it implies."

John believed that if young men and women spent a year in apostolic service, they might be more likely to work full-time for the church, enter the priesthood or religious life, or become committed laity "who see the apostolate as a normal and essential part of life." The greatest percentage would fall into the third category, he admitted, but this was exactly the place where Vatican II said most lay persons should be. A city parish that had 50 to 200 laity who had served the church would have "sparkplugs" and an ideal bridge in overcoming some of the problems of poor communications between clergy and laity. "Certainly the Council's aims for a better liturgy could be carried out more easily with a number of persons like this in each parish," he wrote. "Certainly the catechetical programs would be enriched. Ecumenical work could be carried out with more understanding and greater efficiency."

While criticism of the institutional church would certainly continue, and perhaps it should, John added, there would nevertheless be laity in each parish who would have a better understanding of the day-to-day realities of the church. They would be able to evaluate sensible criticism and to pass it on, and to straighten out misunderstanding occasionally when criticism was made unjustly, based on a poor understanding of the real situation. In the paper, John suggested also taking steps to look for broader recruitment bases and making volunteer service possible for those who did not have a college education. At the time he was initiating a 90-day training period for Hispanics who would serve as volunteers in parishes in the Southwest.

A national training center

During 1966, John was trying also to persuade the officers of Extension to create and fund a national apostolic training and research center primarily concerned with specialized training of laypeople. Some of the center's activities, he suggested in the November 1966 paper, were:

1. Development of the best possible pre-serve training for all Extension Volunteers. This would probably be at least a three-month program.

2. Coordination of in-service training for all volunteers.

3. Special developmental training for volunteers remaining beyond one year, consisting of training periods after each year of service.

4. Highly specialized programs aimed at intensive development of men and women who, having completed their volunteer service, wish to receive additional training so that they may serve full-time in the church as parish workers, Newman workers, catechists and in other apostolic specialties.

5. Training, formation and development programs for parish and community leaders who are not volunteers, but who would benefit from short, intense courses and could take the benefit directly into their home parish or diocese.

John had proposed this idea earlier in an April 1966 paper titled, "Preliminary Thoughts on the Extension Pastoral Institute." He said it was quite widely accepted as fact that the church would not have sufficient priests and religious to carry on its work in the future. "Even if we did have, the new understanding which has come forth from the teachings of Vatican II and the theological writings which went before it and were published during and just after it have made it quite plain that the layman has an indispensable role in God's plan for the salvation of all," he wrote. "It is plain fact and sad fact that laymen are not prepared for this role, rarely even understand what it is."

He saw his vision as not pessimistic, but realistic. "We are living in a very exciting time and there is every indication that the church is able and willing to meet the challenges that it faces. The human resources of the church remain great. General interest in the church is at an all-time high in some ways. Above and beyond all that we have the promise of Christ to be with us until the consummation of the world. We have the grace and power of the Holy Spirit. Still, we could fail. We could fail if we do not begin at once to bring all possible resources to bear on the problem of 'preaching the Gospel to every creature.'" John saw the pastoral institute as a gigantic undertaking, beyond perhaps even his own reach. "That it must be begun, that it must be started soon, that it must be effective, that it must be the best possible operation, all of these things are beyond question," he wrote. "Perhaps we have waited too long. The answer is not in buildings. We already have far too many of those and one of the problems of the future may very well be what to do with them. The answer is in people, in all kinds of people. . . . What we propose to do is to bring not only hope, but ways of converting hope into reality in the very near future."

John noted that such training institutes had already been carried out with success in Germany, France, Belgium and a few other places. He proposed to Extension that the institute be established in connection with Fordham University, with two satellite training centers, to educate not only laity but priests and religious. The executive committee of Extension, however, did not approve his proposal. Instead, funding was provided for scholarships for some who wanted to study at Fordham. "Cardinal Dearden was at the (April 1966) meeting and listened to what I had to say," John recalls. "He recognized that training laity was a continuing problem for each diocese, but thought it should be handled locally. But I was never convinced that every diocese had the resources to do the training that was needed."

Broad-based ministry

Though he admits some mistakes were made, John believes his work with the Extension Volunteers only reinforced his perception of the importance and the potential of broad-based ministry as the basis of Christian community. "God teaches us many of life's important lessons by allowing us to stumble down several dead-ends before we find the right direction. In my work with the volunteers we rushed headlong into many blind alleys," he said in a 1983 talk on lay ministry. "With our eyes wide-shut and armed with the best intentions and enthusiasm, we fell flat on our faces on more than one occasion. At times we would ask too much of people — sending people off to minister for a church they did not know. Sometimes we placed people in situations with inadequate preparation and minimal support. Sometimes we overworked people or, perhaps even more damaging, we underworked people.

"What I witnessed again and again was this dynamic of faith and ministry supporting one another. The more the person developed in his or her ministry, the deeper his or her faith journey. Ministry questions inevitably lead to faith questions and vice versa. Like walking on two feet, belief with action — faith with ministry — was the process which brought the disciples closer to our Lord. I believe it is through ministry that the sacraments of initiation find their fulfillment."

John regrets that at the end of the 1960s the Extension Society concentrated less on recruiting volunteers and more on raising money for needy parishes in mission dioceses. The volunteer program ended in 1971. With Extension's help, the U.S. bishops later created the International Liaison for Lay Volunteers in Mission to connect individuals with volunteer positions in some 200 programs today.

"The campus unrest at that time had something to do with the program's ending," John says. "Many church or government-affiliated service organizations were sort of suspect or not very attractive to young people. The Peace Corps and Vista both experienced this." He adds, "I wish we'd kept our volunteers. It wasn't so much what they did for the church that was important, although it was a real contribution. It was how they were changed by volunteering. They built their own new values. They got a whole new concept of the problems of the church. They saw the limited and often deplorable situation in isolated rural areas. They developed as Christians, doing the work of the Gospel. Doing this broadened their whole faith experience. I know it did for me. Your concept of the church can never be a narrow one again."

Experience shapes their lives

The impact of John Sullivan and the Extension Lay Volunteers continues to be felt in the lives of former volunteers. They in turn continue to have ripple effects on the church by their individual contributions. In 1990, some of the former Extension Volunteers who had given a year or more of service held a reunion in Chicago. Responding to a questionnaire for the reunion, many said their volunteer years came at a pivotal time, a time that continues to shape their lives. A small number continued to work at the very same mission or in the same area, but many more said they are continuing in the same kind of work, especially in Catholic schools. While many said the Extension Volunteer years confirmed the career they had chosen, a good number went back to school to get new degrees and changed careers to get into people-oriented jobs such as teaching, nursing and social work. Even those who now have different kinds of jobs carry over their volunteer values into their present jobs. Many said volunteering became a continuous way of life.

Peter Gallagher, of Ossining, New York, calls John "an extraordinary man who has had a profound impact on my life. . . . He loved God as intensely as anyone I have ever met. He always had time for individual people and their cares and problems. He had a well-developed sense of humor and could tell a joke as well as any stand-up comedian. He was loyal and generous."

At age 27 in 1962-63, Gallagher worked with John on publicity and recruitment in Extension's Chicago office. "I wasn't the typical volunteer," Gallagher says. "I traveled to 26 states. I helped produce a half-hour movie on the volunteers. I had by-lined articles in major Catholic publications. I edited a newsletter that went out to volunteers and prospects. I appeared on local radio and TV shows. . . . What a great opportunity this was for someone who liked this kind of thing — and could do it for a cause. . . . All this was going on while my volunteer colleagues served as teachers, nurses and catechists out in the field. How I sometimes envied them. I thought, 'What the hell am I doing in a suit and tie in downtown Chicago when I volunteered for a post in the boondocks?' But that's where Sully wanted me."

Gallagher, who now works for a consulting firm that provides advice on fundraising campaigns to nonprofit clients, concludes: "My days with the Extension Lay Volunteers were full, obviously, but I loved what I was doing. I felt I was making a difference, affecting people's lives. I felt good about myself and the world. I had time to think, to reflect, to focus on what was really important. And there was no looking back. What motivated me then motivates me now. My decision to join the volunteers and my year of service was a turning point in my life. I shall never forget Father Sullivan and his sincerity and dedication to the cause of the home missions."

Kay Derner Brown came from St. Peter, Minnesota, to work as a volunteer in Oklahoma from 1964-65. She still lives in Harrah, Oklahoma, and works as a school counselor. Volunteering "changed my entire life," she says. "When I came to Oklahoma, I had never met a Baptist or a black. It was a big shock to me that everything didn't close down during Holy Week like it did at home. But I liked the openness of the church in Oklahoma. The laity had such an important role. Extension broadened my horizons, and having a foot in both Minnesota and Oklahoma has made me more tolerant of differences in people and cultures."

Veronica Carroll Donnelly, originally a New Yorker who now lives in Tulsa, served as a volunteer in Puerto Rico from 1963-65. "My experience set in motion a lifetime of volunteer work for others," she assesses. Her volunteer years were "exciting, challenging and humbling." Mary Anne Slattery, now a district attorney in Wyandotte County, Kansas, was a volunteer in Texas and then recruited for Extension from 1965-67. Because of John's confidence in her, she says, "I was able to reach beyond myself. It's something you didn't realize until years later, but that support and affirmation gave you the courage to move on."

Filled with energy and spirit

An English teacher at a Catholic high school in New York City, Teresita Dwyer O'Leary recalls her volunteer years (summers of 1961-62 in Oklahoma and 1963-65 in Colorado) as "being filled with energy and spirit and wanting to change the world. We were at the height of an idealistic time in our lives and believed we could be agents of change. I felt I was a vital part of the community. I had hope that the church was changing and that women and laity in general would be more dynamically involved."

She adds: "Those years and the experience changed my life. I became more compassionate and understanding of different people. I broke out of a very secure and limited social circle. I became a teacher and have spent my career teaching at-risk populations on a wide range of levels."

Elizabeth McMahon Jeep, now a religious educator and writer, was one of the first recruited from Manhattanville College by John for the Oklahoma volunteers. She was later part of the Extension Volunteers' training team. Her volunteer years were "wonderful, happy and hopeful — part of the spirit of renewal and deepening in the church, before fear and exaggeration and reaction set in. It was a taste of what true community and liturgy and leadership might look like in a church moved by the spirit and by faith," she says. Her experience "is a vision that has fed my imagination and kept hope alive and nourished a sense of perspective and a sense of humor. Many who lived through the 1960s — as volunteers or not — became cynical. I chose to remain hopeful."

Jim White, an Extension Volunteer in the late 1960s who later started a Catholic Worker house in Kansas City, Missouri, calls the volunteers' effort simply ministry in service. "There was great political ferment at the time, and the volunteers were taught we have a responsibility and an obligation to transform and heal society," he says. "I enjoyed doing this and felt useful. I just continued doing that throughout my life. That's probably what some would call a career."

The Extension Lay Volunteers during the turbulent 1960s helped to prove that "there are not two churches — clergy and laity. There is one church of Christ with different functions, a variety of gifts of the Spirit," John said in his homily at the volunteers' 1990 reunion. "The mission of the church is a twofold mission — to join every woman, man and child to God and to shape this earth into a city of justice and peace, a city of love."

CHAPTER FOUR

At the Madalene: First Experience
With Team Ministry

FRESH FROM HIS WORK WITH THE EXTENSION LAY VOLUNTEERS, John returned to Tulsa in the summer of 1968 to become pastor of the Church of the Madalene. Bishop Reed also appointed him episcopal vicar for the eastern part of the Diocese of Oklahoma City and Tulsa. He served as a member of the Pastoral Board (of laity and priests) that was established at the behest of the Diocesan Pastoral Council — Oklahoma's was the first such body in the country to advise Bishop Reed on a weekly basis.

The Second Vatican Council had extended through the central period (1962-1965) of Bishop Reed's episcopacy. The council experience firmed up the notion in Bishop Reed's mind that the church was undergoing a crisis of growth and must suffer a sweeping renewal. Father David Monahan, in his written history of the church in Oklahoma,[1] notes that although not an ideological liberal, Bishop Reed was a liberal in the sense of being unfettered by prejudices himself and desiring to give others the freedom of initiative. Thus he opted for the free-spirited *Oklahoma Courier* newspaper, lay

---

1. "One Family: One Century," A Photographic History of the Catholic Church in Oklahoma 1875-1975.

involvement through the Diocesan Pastoral Council, promotion of civil rights and liturgical relevancy.

The combination of Bishop Reed's openness to new ideas, the conviction that changes were needed, and a difficulty in saying "no" made Bishop Reed's later years filled with tension and harassment, Father Monahan writes. There was an alarming exodus of Oklahoma priests from the active ministry. If he felt the situation was partly out of control or that the pressures were intolerable, he rarely if ever showed it. "Nothing would disturb Bishop Reed," John recalls. "He was a very gentle man. He was the most charitable man I ever knew. He was one of the first bishops to speak out against the Vietnam War. . . . We had many priests who were well-educated and were speaking out on social issues and the civil rights movement. Bishop Reed was intelligent and honest enough to take some unpopular positions."

Within the Oklahoma Catholic clergy there had run for a long time a strong strain of liberalism, Father Monahan notes. Bishop Reed's tenure, coinciding with the dynamics surrounding Vatican II, brought the liberal movement from theory to practice within the church in Oklahoma. The liberal movement appeared in many different forms: ecumenism (Tulsa's Madalene Church was the first Catholic parish in the nation to join the Council of Churches), liturgical innovation (a point of considerable tension between Bishop Reed and his priests), and the establishment of two experimental parishes (the Community of John XXIII in Oklahoma City and the Church of the Living Christ in Tulsa). Critical reaction to the liberal activity varied from somewhat disturbed to loud outrage. More than once Bishop Reed's residence was picketed in protest to happenings in the diocese. Bishop Reed lived out his final years in a swirl of controversy. He died suddenly of a heart attack on Sept. 8, 1971.

Great sense of loyalty

Among the Oklahoma priests, "John was unique because of his great sense of loyalty to the church," says Father Dennis Dorney. As a newly ordained priest in July 1968, he was assigned as John's associate pastor at the Church of the Madalene and worked with him for four-and-a-half years. "Some of the more progressive priests wanted change too fast and without much forethought. John had the ability and a vision to call the church beyond where it was, and yet that sense of patience to work with what was to make that vision a reality. This was not a quality which was present in every Oklahoma priest, but I found it in him." He adds, "As a young priest, I noticed that he had a profound love of the priesthood very present in his life, which led him to work with many men who were struggling with their commitment. He would often go to men who had left the priesthood and invite them to return. He not only talked about these things, but he dedicated himself to living them out."

John's pastoral team at the Madalene included Father Dorney, Father Thomas Biller, Benedictine Sisters Barbara Austin and Marie Pierre Fleming, Sister Joanne Gehling (a member of the Franciscan Sisters of Perpetual Adoration), and Frank O'Meara. In 1970, John closed the parish school and developed a comprehensive ministry plan. It included an active religious education program for children, teenagers and adults in the 900-family parish. This "team ministry" approach, as he calls it, evolved out of his previous pastoral experiences and his work with the Extension Volunteers. "I always wanted to pursue this idea because, as Archbishop Paul Hallinan (of Atlanta, Georgia) had said, the purse strings and personnel determine the priorities. We were doing less and less for more people, and more and more for less people," John recalls. "The school was going bankrupt, and I made the prudential judgment that if we closed it we could do more for the parish. Some people thought that when I closed the school it was the end of the parish. That was a common forecast. But on the contrary, in the months following the closing, the parish income increased, which was the acid test."

The religious education program, which ran all year long, was directed by O'Meara, who had a doctorate from the Institut Catòlique in Paris and had been referred to John by Christianne Brusselmanns of Louvain University in Belgium. The school classrooms were converted into 10 "living rooms" to give the education classes a homelike atmosphere, John says. Each room had four tables and seven students at each table. There were four catechists, one at each table, and a lead catechist. The catechists came a half-hour before class to review the day's lesson and stayed after class to prepare for the next. Nurses were hired to provide care for the babies of the catechists.

"We had 600 kids in parish religious education. In the summers we had large numbers of college and high school students and we had films and discussions," John remembers. "We had beautiful liturgies planned for children. We discovered that sacramental programs, if they were well done, were very attractive. We got 90% of the parents involved. The teachers' training program was a very effective means for adult education. We planned 30 Thursday evenings on the *Dutch Catechism.* Then we discovered it was the same 150 people coming all the time — we were making saints of the saints. So we cut the sessions down to four. It was something — it was really perfect. I never wanted to leave there."

John adds, "I was so blessed with a talented parish staff. We'd go out into the neighborhoods, and we'd know everybody and everything about the families. The sisters started visiting hospital patients and people accepted this new role. I knew we had all the ingredients for success. The underlying idea was to provide quality religious education and ministry to everyone in the parish. I couldn't ever understand why that couldn't be duplicated elsewhere."

John was the glue

John "was excited about the Madalene, had lots of ideas and vision, and he tried to make all of us on the parish team a part of this," says Father Dorney. "He threw a lot of responsibilities at me that someone else might not have given to someone newly ordained. I think it all goes back to one of his famous sayings — that it upset him when people left the Catholic Church, and he lost sleep if they left out of an ignorance of their own faith. This is why he wanted to build a religious education program that was high quality and professional, to offer young people and adults the best we could in their faith. John was the glue that held all this together. He was truly visionary about where the church should be, and there's an excitement that goes with being part of that that's really contagious."

For the most part the reaction of parishioners was favorable, adds Father Dorney. "The lack of reception was mainly on the part of those who still felt hurt about the school's closing. That was a somewhat strong group of people. Part of that sentiment was neutralized because we had an agreement with the neighboring parish, St. Pius X, that our children could attend at the in-parish tuition rate and the Madalene would subsidize their tuition. A large number sent their children to St. Pius X."

John was convinced that closing the Madalene school would make the parish's ministry stronger, says Mary Agnes Sullivan, John's sister-in-law. She and John's brother, Dan, a legal aid attorney, and their children, were members of the parish. "John was thinking about how best to serve everyone," she recalls. "By closing one school, he could make another (St. Pius) stronger. Some people obviously thought he was wrong, but later were still very loving and loyal supporters of John."

Father Biller, who has multiple sclerosis and came to live at the Madalene in 1970, recalls that John was instrumental in getting priests, sisters and laypeople working together in religious education. "I always saw his work as a pastor in Oklahoma and with the Extension Volunteers as having a great impact on his philosophy," he says. "The Madalene was one of the first parishes to hire a full-time religious education director. It was a natural phenomenon for John that women religious and laity became more involved. He saw clearly the role of men and women in the church, and he didn't have much tension with the roles."

'Our work came to fruition'

As a young religious woman, Sister Barbara Austin came to work at the Madalene from 1968 to 1975. John had baptized her as an infant in Guthrie, and she had known him ever since. "There couldn't have been a more collaborative parish staff than ours," she contends. "We met every week and were involved in all that went on. There were other parishes employing women religious, but ours was the only one I was aware of that had the kind of team approach we did."

The pastoral team divided the parish into districts, with one team member responsible for the families in each district. "At least four of us would be in every religious education class — one team leader joined by parishioners who were co-leaders. It was ongoing education from preschool through adulthood," says Sister Barbara, who is now vocation director for her Benedictine community and a campus minister at Tulsa University. "The marvelous part was that people who were co-leaders eventually took over the leadership at The Madalene. Now those people are in key roles throughout the Diocese of Tulsa. And they went through this formation more than 20 years ago. Our work really came to fruition."

Sister Barbara describes John as "very collaborative, yet very much directive about what he wanted done in the parish. We all did our own programming in family education, and he allowed us this freedom and encouraged us. He always wanted to be part of the experience and to know what was going on in people's lives. His primary goal was education and formation of the laity — a total community kind of approach. It's something that's still controversial — some people have responded positively and some have not."

Appointed a bishop

Sister Barbara says John's approach to ministry made him a popular priest in Tulsa. His appointment on July 25, 1972, by Pope Paul VI to succeed Bishop John L. Paschang as the bishop of Grand Island, Nebraska, left him with a variety of conflicting feelings. "My dominant feelings at this time are of a keen awareness of my own limitations and inadequacies in assuming this office, as well as a tremendous sense of dependence on the goodness of God and the prayers of friends," John said in a written statement. "In all candor, I am grieved at the prospect of leaving the Oklahoma priests and nuns and brothers who have been my closest friends and associates for so many years, leaving my family and the people of Oklahoma, and especially the parishioners of Madalene Parish. But in a spirit of faith and obedience and with great hope, I look forward to this new responsibility."

He added: "My expectations are great and, I believe, realistic because I have known Bishop Paschang, and from a distance I have observed him and his labors in Western Nebraska and have always considered him to be a pastorally minded bishop. No doubt the resources of the Diocese of Grand Island today, in terms of the faith of the people and the quality of the priests and religious, are due in great part to the example and leadership of Bishop Paschang. Being a bishop and the ordinary of a diocese in these times is an awesome responsibility, and I will come to the Diocese of Grand Island with a heartfelt petition for your prayers and support."

John's consecration as the fifth bishop of Grand Island drew a large crowd to ceremonies in the Tulsa Assembly Center on Sept. 19, 1972. John requested the ceremony be held in the Assembly Center so that everyone who wished might be present for the rites, especially school children. Several thousand people attended, as did 32 archbishops, bishops and abbots, and some 250 priests from Oklahoma, Nebraska and other states. It marked the first time a consecration in Oklahoma was held outside a cathedral. Cardinal John Cody of Chicago, chancellor of the Catholic Church Extension Society, presided at the ceremonies, while Bishop John R. Quinn, who had been appointed bishop of Oklahoma City and Tulsa in 1971, was the chief consecrator. The principal co-consecrators were Bishop Charles Buswell of Pueblo, Colorado, a fellow Oklahoman, and John's close friend, Bishop John May, who had been named bishop of Mobile, Alabama in 1969.

Inside the Assembly Center, a 16-by-32-foot banner of white with red and gold lettering bore the legend of John's episcopacy: "Come, Lord Jesus." His chosen motto, an ancient liturgical expression which looks forward to the coming of Christ in glory, was also his prayer that the spirit of Jesus might pervade all the actions of people.

CHAPTER FIVE

Diocese of Grand Island: Team Ministry Flourishes

CARDINAL JOHN CODY, ARCHBISHOP OF CHICAGO, PRESIDED AT installation ceremonies for John in St. Mary's Cathedral in Grand Island on Sept. 21, 1972. Some 250 priests and more than 100 women religious attended the ceremonies.

In his installation homily, John set the tone for his efforts in Grand Island by emphasizing pastoral ministry and witness. "A bishop is called to teach, to sanctify and to govern, but the Second Vatican Council reminds every bishop that he is to 'stand in the midst of his people as one who serves,'" John said. "I do not call you servants, I call you my friends and I am called to be your servant. . . . As individuals, and as a faith community, we are called to bear witness to the good news of Christ; to make the unity for which Christ prayed a reality; and to make our lives an incarnation of the love of Christ by unselfish service of human need wherever it may be found."

John stressed to Catholics that they had something vital to say to the men and women of their time. "Some of us may do it by preaching and the pastoral ministry; all of us must do it by the witness of our lives . . . It is up to you and to me to preach the Gospel, to bear witness to the reasons we have for living and hoping." He noted that education in the Catholic faith for both children and adults was a major responsibility for every bishop, as prescribed by Vatican II's Decree on Bishops.

Priority is people

The only one possible priority for a bishop is people, John said. "Our institutions, our pastoral programs, our preaching and ministry make no sense if they are not animated by a totally unselfish desire to serve the real needs of people. We, as a church, must incarnate the love of Christ. . . . We must make our love real in our families, in our parishes, in our towns, recognizing the love of Christ in our neighbor, especially the poor, the lonely and the suffering."

John's was the largest diocese (by square miles) in Nebraska, covering an area from Grand Island west to the Wyoming border. It contained 44,000 square miles, with a Catholic population of nearly 50,000 (out of a total population of more than 200,000), centered primarily around the city of Grand Island. The diocese, established in 1910, had some 50 parishes and 40 missions. Of the more than 60 active priests in the diocese, one third were born and raised in the small towns of Greeley, Spaulding, and O'Connor — from a county nicknamed "The Holy Land," settled by Irish and German immigrants in the late 19th century. The small area also accounted for many vocations to religious life. Many of the people in the diocese were farmers, ranchers, and suppliers of services and equipment for these two key occupations.

"One of the most important things to me was that we had an excellent group of priests in the diocese," John says. "The family life was also very healthy. And we had many native sons and daughters of Nebraska who were in religious life. Bishop Paschang had done a tremendous job of implementing the Vatican II reforms among the people. He was a very pastoral bishop and very much loved."

Carrying the team ministry approach with him from The Church of the Madalene in Tulsa, John wanted to make available trained ministers to every parish in the far-flung diocese. Grand Island was "an ideal place to try and expand the team ministry concept," he recalls. "People were still feeling their way about comprehensive ministry in many respects. I wanted to meet the parishes' needs in spite of their distances. About 10 parishes were over 300 miles from my house, and one parish was almost 400. So if I went out for a pastoral visit on a weekend, it might be 700 miles driving."

Recruits women religious

For the team ministry, John personally invited 30 to 40 women religious in the diocese and from other parts of the country — and from several religious orders — to apply for the job of pastoral associate and to serve in the parishes of the diocese. The response of the women religious was positive and immediate, says Sister Judy Warmbold, who met John shortly after he became bishop. (John had previously met with Sister Judy's superior, Sister Josephine Oldani, in Denver.) She met with John in North Platte, Nebraska, on behalf of her community, the Daughters of Charity (St. Louis province). The community was looking to place sisters in dioceses with unmet needs.

"I'll never forget that meeting," Sister Judy remembers. "Bishop Sullivan had this dream and this vision and he just put it all together that day. He took us over to meet Msgr. (Lawrence) Portrey at St. Patrick's Parish. He said he'd need to get four automobiles for our sisters to work there. I almost fell off my chair. Somebody who would have this vision that all four sisters would need an automobile was unusual. And he talked health insurance and other benefits for us. Then he took us to look at some housing. By the time the day was finished, we had the whole plan in motion."

Within a month, four Daughters of Charity were ready to work in the diocese, Sister Judy recalls. "We arrived in

North Platte to a diocesan meeting where John called together 30 or so women religious from many communities — this whole crowd that he had recruited," she says. "They were going to be on pastoral teams all over the diocese. We all sat in a circle; none of us knew each other. And in his inimitable way, he went around the circle and introduced every single person."

She adds, "At that point, it (the team ministry) was tantamount to a revolution in pastoral ministry, because very few of these women religious had ever worked in parishes. We were all coming out of teaching in the schools and other institutional ministries. And the priests we were working with had never had women on their staffs. So it was a major shakeup of the diocese."

Needs of the people

John laid out the team ministry concept idea initially to the priests' senate. He proposed that for the pastoral good of the people the experiment should be tried. He considered the several possible difficulties with the clergy, listened to their doubts, but sold most of the priests on the idea that the personnel of the diocese should be used in the best possible way — and that the needs of the people and of the church were paramount. The Grand Island priests, for the most part, agreed to give it their best. Even though they had not been trained for this type of team ministry, they would be willing to learn. John left his door open for the settling of difficulties and to be of assistance along the way.

The team ministry "opened up a lot of the ministries the priests had been doing to more interaction with more people," recalls Father Charles Torpey, who in 1973 was serving as associate pastor at Blessed Sacrament Parish in the city of Grand Island. "In some ways the teams were not all that successful at first, but the effect of having the teams started was significant. There was some skepticism among the priests, but mostly it was a spirit or feeling that the bishop wants to do this and we would certainly be willing to do it. They were trying to understand the concept he wanted."

John's idea was "to put one priest out there and give him the support so that the pastoral work could be done," says Father James O'Kane, whom John appointed in 1973 as pastor of a new parish, St. Leo's, in Grand Island. "The team ministry was a large difference in direction from what we'd had before. It also coincided with the opening of three new parishes in the diocese."

The priests' reaction to team ministry was mixed, he adds. "I personally loved it. The people on my team complemented each other. Some of the priests did not always receive the concept so well. They were put off and intimidated by it. It was just contrary to the style they'd always known. Most of the people in the parishes loved the idea. In parishes where the pastor didn't like the idea, there were mixed reviews by the people. All I knew was John's vision was right. And this is why he felt compelled to have continuing education for the priests so they would understand that vision. I felt his rationale was not simply based on the shortage of priests, but that people could bring their different gifts to ministry — that parish ministry could be much more broad than it was previously."

Team ministry launched

The team ministry was actually launched on Labor Day in 1973 when 31 women religious joined 21 diocesan priests in the formation of new pastoral teams to serve in 15 parishes. They met for a workshop at the Ramada Inn in North Platte and heard speakers of national stature express their admiration and enthusiasm for the project. The team ministry had already received considerable national attention, especially in the Catholic press. A Sept. 14, 1973 article in *The National Catholic Reporter* called it the "most ambitious U.S. program involving religious women in pastoral roles."

Auxiliary Bishop George Evans of Denver, who had directed the use of women religious in pastoral roles in his archdiocese, called the Grand Island program "monumental" in comparison to the way Denver's began. Another speaker at the workshop, Sister Ellen Louise Burns, from the campus ministry team at Rockhurst College in Kansas City, Missouri, said the team ministry effort was the "best thing that's happened in pastoral work in five years."

John said he was restraining his enthusiasm about the project because he knew there were risks involved, and that the program would be watched critically. At the same time, his determination that the program succeed was very evident. "I expect great things of you," he said to members of the teams. "In a way, we are pioneers and the entire church will be watching our progress." In his homily at Mass during the workshop, he recalled a priest he once knew who "when he bought a new car, took every bit of chrome off it. He had a room in his house full of chrome. When asked why, he said it was his way of rebelling against car designers telling him what his car should be like. There is a point in this for us. You in pastoral ministry need to act according to what the Gospel asks of you, and not according to what someone in the world expects of you."

John's intent was to keep the job descriptions of the pastoral teams loose and flexible. He said the task of the teams would be to determine the needs of the people in their areas and then fill them with a wide variety of ministries. Some would work in newly consolidated mission parishes. John said, for example, that a team of "one-and-a-half" priests and two nuns would work with six small parishes spread out over a large area. He believed that consolidation would help young priests. He noted there were a number of parishes with only 60 or so families, and that this was not enough of a challenge for a young priest. Each priest would now be working with several hundred families. Women religious would be involved in home nursing, work with the elderly, social action programs, education and other areas. Most important, John said he wanted the pastoral teams to bring more personal contact with the church to a great number of people in the diocese.

Dominican Sister Regina McCarthy, a native of Greeley, Nebraska, was a member of the pastoral team in North Platte for five years. The team included four priests and several sisters, including Sister Judy Warmbold, who was co-director of religious education with Sister Regina at St. Patrick's Parish. "We started the whole team ministry with some trepidation," Sister Regina recalls. "We began with a census of the Catholic population of the entire city. That got us into the households and to know people. We did lots of hospital visits in those early days. My personal interest was in the Hispanic community, so I worked a great deal with Mexican American people."

Long-term effects

Sister Regina, who is now director of Hispanic ministry in the Grand Island diocese, says the team effort was successful and has had long-term effects. John was "so adamant about pastoral ministry for women religious because he was so aware of what he would call the faceless people, the people who were little known in parishes. He wanted these people to become more active, involved and connected to the parishes . . . He believed the church really happens at the parish level. The most impressive thing to me was that he was so conscious of people who might not be noticed normally. He was most approachable and you could count on him to be there. He believed that anytime you can make people realize they're important, then you can minister." In addition, John had "a true belief in women's roles in the church. I think that belief rubbed off on some of the clergy."

The only lay member of the first pastoral teams was Karen (Domandle) Meyerott, serving St. Mary's Cathedral in Grand Island. She had already been working with several parishes in the city in music and liturgy before John approached her about the team ministry. "The first year was a struggle," she remembers. "John assigned us to teams and each was to work out its own vision. He left that in our hands, which was both good and bad. It was a whole new concept for many of the priests. And John expected the priests to be involved. Some teams worked, some didn't, some stayed, and some fell apart. We knew John was a visionary person and this was a challenge to a lot of people.

"As I look back on it today, I believe you have to be a visionary to go along with a visionary," she adds. "That was the real struggle. There was a cross section of personalities on the teams and some didn't know what they were getting into. . . . He wanted to see the diocese involve as many lay people as possible. With me, he was really excited that I was enthused about being involved. He never questioned my ability. If anyone was dedicated and interested, they were welcome."

Real community

Patty Waltemath, who served on the pastoral team with Sister Judy and Sister Regina at St. Patrick's, calls the team ministry "the forerunner of the small Christian communities we see now in the church. It was my first experience of real community. We worked, played and prayed together. We met and shared at our staff meetings what was going on at work and in our lives. It was a very spiritual experience for most everyone who worked on the team."

With the pastoral teams, John's "vision was that people are important, that people have many needs, and we need to try a different approach," assesses Sister Judy Warmbold. "The different approach was that we need men and women ministers ministering to the people. And we need to develop the gifts of the laity. At that point in the early 1970s, he was not recruiting many laypeople to be on the teams. He was recruiting women religious, but his vision was we're going to train the laypeople of each parish and broaden the approach of ministry. He knew we needed to minister to the elderly and the youth — in Catholic schools and in public schools. What he said then was what he always says now: there's only two things that matter, people and the relationships between people. That, in a nutshell, is his vision."

Implementing reforms

Concurrent with the team ministry thrust, John attempted extensive implementation of the reforms of Vatican II in liturgy, sacramental rites and religious education, working in part through an active priests' senate and sisters' council in the diocese. Sister Judy recalls several two-day diocesan events held at the Holiday Inn in North Platte, where clergy, religious and laity (many on the pastoral teams) heard speakers such as noted religious educator Christianne Brusselmanns and Scripture scholar Father Raymond Brown. Not long after he became bishop, John phoned Father Brown to invite him to come and speak to the diocesan priests. Father Brown later wrote to John in July 1977 (upon his appointment as bishop of Kansas City-St. Joseph) and recalled, "Your interest in the continuing education of your priests is something I have not forgotten. . . . You see, I do remember my one and only visit to Nebraska."

Father O'Kane, who served as president of the priests' senate, recalls close cooperation between John and the senate. John attended all senate meetings and participated, because he wanted the senate to play a critical role in deciding how the diocese should or should not move. "One of the most important things John did was to start the continuing education of priests' committee," recalls Father O'Kane, who is now pastor of St. Mary's Cathedral in Grand Island. "This was probably the biggest outward sign of what he did with the priests' senate. We always had two continuing education sessions each year, one in the spring and one in the fall. He brought in prominent speakers and spent a lot of money doing this, because he was convinced that if you get the information out to people, if you form them, you can have the kind of diocese you want. He had a lot of challenge from some of the older priests. But today it has really paid dividends, because we can look back on those times and we are a well-formed diocese as far as our priests are concerned."

"I heard John say often that he wanted to provide people in the parishes with the best kind of ministry they could have, with all the opportunities for sacramental life, for education, and for participating in the life of the church," remembers Father Bernard Berger, former editor of the diocesan newspaper, *The West Nebraska Register*. "Those few priests who resisted John's efforts reacted that way more because they disagreed with the updating called for by Vatican II."

Updating religious education

Father Torpey, who was in charge of priests' continuing education and the diocesan worship commission, contends that "part of it was motivated by John's desire to implement Vatican II, but the main motivation was that he wanted to focus on updating the religious education programs in the diocese. And he wanted to get more people involved in ministry. He wanted people to have some exposure and training so they could do this. I remember him telling us at a priests' meeting that he kind of had a moment of awareness of what he really thought the church should do. He could see that we just needed to get more laypeople involved in the ministry of the church."

Fathers Torpey and O'Kane, as well as laywoman Maureen Kelly, whom John had hired as diocesan director of religious education, traveled to 23 areas of the diocese in the fall of 1975 to give a complete explanation and demonstration of the new rite of reconciliation. Kelly was one of only a few laywomen at the time to serve in such a diocesan role. "I was amazed when I first met John and he told me his ideas about lay ministry," she recalls. "He saw the importance of religious education for everyone. Shortly after I met him, I thought, 'I would go to the wall for this man.' And my experience working with him was the same. I was in my early thirties and it was my first positive experience of collaboration."

In meetings with the Diocesan Sisters' Council in 1972 and 1973, John made it clear that he saw the need of such an organization of sisters as a means of championing their rights. He spoke of the need of providing sisters with proper retirement and education. He also recognized the need of fostering vocations. "We're treading water!" he said at one meeting. "We have to go the other way . . . We are so fortunate. There is nothing we can't do if we want to." Sister Judy Warmbold recalls the sisters' council as a strong network of women religious. "We all knew each other, even though the diocese was such a vast territory. It was an *esprit de corps* of women and it was very active."

Assessed his efforts

In an interview with *The West Nebraska Register* on his third anniversary as bishop in August 1975, John assessed his efforts, including the establishment of three new parishes. In 1973, John had approved the new parishes of St. Leo in southwest Grand Island, the Church of the Resurrection in northwest Grand Island, and Holy Spirit Parish in North Platte. "People inquire about priorities, and I would simply say our priority in this diocese is simply the constant improvement or perfection of ministry, of the manner in which the church serves," John noted in the interview. He cited his greatest single disappointment as "my inability to have the priests, sisters and laity assume more responsibility in pastoral planning and decision making. In many places we do not have parish councils and we do not have a diocesan council." His second greatest disappointment was his "inability to win the confidence of all our people and to secure the cooperation that we must have in the mission we share. One example of this is my plea for parents to enroll their children in our Catholic schools — especially junior and senior high."

John added, "It is very important that our people and I know one another personally . . . Then, hopefully, we can enjoy true unity and a great sensitivity to the needs of one another in the diocese and of people outside our population."

Painful decision

In February 1975, John decided to close two elementary schools in the city of Grand Island (St. Mary's Cathedral School and Blessed Sacrament School) at the end of that school year, and to keep open a junior/senior high school, Central Catholic. It was a painful decision for John and one that also caused a good deal of controversy. In October 1972, John had met with the clergy in the city of Grand Island and was told that the diocese would have to contribute $114,000 to keep all three schools operating. "This situation was not new, and there had been a substantial operating deficit for some years," even before St. Leo's and Resurrection parishes were opened, John noted in a Nov. 5, 1973 press statement. "Later, I discovered 100% of the total Sunday contributions in Grand Island could not cover the reported school expense," he added. "The diocese could not possibly continue this practice because, in justice, we have schools in other towns and even some very worthy missions in the diocese that would also have a claim on these funds and we could be bankrupt in a month. With the new parishes, with better service given to all our people in Grand Island, I believe we have among other things the only possible solution to the school problem (if there is one) . . . Even in these times of shared decision making, so often the final word is left to the bishop, but in this school question the people truly make the decision by enrolling their children and by supporting the schools financially. That is the crux of the decision."

To advise him on the schools, John set up a committee, which in December 1974 offered him only one recommendation: maintaining a kindergarten-through-12th-grade school system. In his view the committee did not provide a realistic plan for supporting such a program. He was most concerned that the recommendation made no provision for payment of the Central Catholic High School loan, which amounted to $50,000 annually. "We are in an extremely difficult position as we are confronted with an intolerable and constantly increasing operating deficit, and some decision has to be made," John noted in a column in the diocesan newspaper. He contended that there were pressing reasons for retaining Central Catholic High School including: lack of an adequate and viable religious education program on the junior/senior level for public school children; younger children receive more home and parental guidance than adolescents; and it would be much easier to reopen elementary schools than a high school if needed in future years.

The advisory committee "made an emotional rather than a reasonable decision," assesses Father O'Kane. "Because they were indecisive, John as bishop had to be decisive. What he wrestled with was how to use the diocesan money and parish staff people to give good religious education to youngsters at an age when they were not alienated from their parents and when teachers were not intimidated. He wanted to bolster the early childhood education programs in each parish and keep the junior/senior high school open to influence adolescents. Unfortunately, for some people, all John was known for was his closing of the grade schools. That limited in a real way his effectiveness as bishop. But the fact was he was doing them a service."

A question of impact

"It was a very tense and tough time" for John, adds Father Berger. "There was a great deal of resistance and anger from the people, and even today that lingers somewhat. It was a question of impact: could there be more impact upon the faith and growth of religious knowledge by retaining the grade schools? At the time, I wrote an editorial in the newspaper supporting his decision. I wrote that he listened to the advice of the committee, but it was his choice not to take their advice. It was one of those cases where only time would vindicate whether the decision was the right thing to do."

Seven months after his "regretful but necessary" decision to close the grade schools, John said in *The West Nebraska Register* interview, "I continue to receive occasional letters of protest and I know some people will go to their graves convinced that this decision was wrong and unnecessary. However, in general, the reaction after the initial and terrible shock has been positive and supportive."

He added, "I detest turmoil and dissension, but if it can be productive, I am willing to endure it. From this episode, I see parents of younger children assuming greater responsibility, with the assistance of our sisters, and the parishes being compelled to have . . . superior religious education programs. I also see Central Catholic High School's future secure, and our total educational commitment in Grand Island being defined for years to come." Later, in 1977, John would reflect that "I personally feel that the only way we can save our schools is by utilizing all other ministries."

National recognition

Outside the Grand Island diocese, John received the respect of his fellow bishops by being named chairman of the American Board of Catholic Missions and for serving for nine years on the National Conference of Catholic Bishops' Committee for Liaison with the Leadership Conference of Women Religious. He was also a member of the bishops' committees on the laity and for Latin America, and on the bishops' administrative board. The invitation to serve on the LCWR liaison committee was extremely attractive, he said, because "a large share of the church's future is in the hands of religious women. They need all the encouragement and

backing they can possibly be afforded . . . The formation of
their members presents communities with a large challenge,
because ministries have broadened and preparation for these
ministries must be adequate."

By the summer of 1975, John was ready to evaluate the
pastoral team ministry effort across the diocese. He worked
out an agreement with the Glenmary Research Center for
researcher David M. Byers to "describe the rationale, background and accomplishments of the pastoral ministry program and, with the help of the participants, put the challenges, opportunities and issues in focus." The planned
study consisted of field interviews (in October-November
1975), an analysis of these interviews, a two-day meeting between researchers and participants (in March 1976) and a
formal written report issued May 1, 1976. The report noted
that despite the failure of a few teams, innovative parish
ministry as a whole had thriven in the diocese, not only in
terms of quality of service but in terms of number of participants and geographic coverage. At the time of the study, 32
priests, 49 sisters and two laywomen were active on teams,
serving the needs of 22 parishes and one mission, out of a
total of 53 parishes in the diocese.

A *dynamic institution*

The report noted, "It is fair to say that the rationale
behind the program is a vision of the church as a dynamic
institution present and active in people's lives. Bishop Sullivan is fond of saying things like 'the church has become the
chaplain of the saved.' He is interested in seeing the parishes reach out to anonymous people whom the institutional
church has so often passed by — the elderly, the shut-in, the
minority person, the lax Catholic, the non-Catholic. And he
feels that all the people deserve the opportunity to learn
their faith from qualified ministers and to get the help
needed to live it."

Although the report cited improved religious education and better sacramental preparation in the teams' parishes, it noted that few team members interviewed included ministry to other Christians or the unchurched in their list of successes. "When one considers that the 49,400 Catholics in the diocese live among 140,600 other Christians and 90,300 unchurched persons, this relative lack of attention to those outside the fold looms as a significant omission in a program which has entered its third year of operation," the report said. It also noted that team support and intra-team relationships were "a gray area," and that some portion of the laity still had little understanding of the team ministry effort.

In another more informal evaluation of the team effort, well-known Chicago priest Msgr. John J. Egan, head of the Catholic Committee on Urban Ministry, cited the positive effects of the laity's acceptance of the program, and that the hard work and dedication of the sisters had won over the majority of the clergy. "Not all of the situations or personnel have worked as planned," he wrote, "but after some adjustments of original perception, and the smoothing out of 'roles,' the sisters' relationship to both clergy and people has been edifying and has added both efficiency and depth to the Catholic ministry in western Nebraska."

Msgr. Egan identified an emerging need for an overall supervisor of the team ministry project, apart from John, to relieve him of the burden and to provide training in interpersonal relationships and pastoral skills for both sisters and clergy. He wrote, "Some sisters, moving from school work into a parochial assignment, find difficulty in working in an uncontrolled situation and the 'delightful confusion' of parish work unsettling. As with the clergy, there is the great need for support systems and affirmation in order to accept failure, compromise, and to understand the insecurity and nitty-gritty of parish work . . . Everything may not be perfect in Grand Island, but they (the bishop and parish teams) know that a start on something exciting in the church has been made. The parish teams have the allegiance and support of the people. They, with the leadership of the bishop, have not been afraid to take a risk for the pastoral good of the entire church."

A new phenomenon

Because parish team ministry was a new phenomenon, both successes and failures were experienced, says Karen Meyerott. "Some of the frustration I heard was that Bishop John did not give a lot of one-two-three directions on how to do parish ministry. Some felt he should have had a more concrete vision of what he wanted us to do and that he left us kind of dangling. It's true that he didn't put his entire vision down on a piece of paper. But he also wanted to leave the idea wide open and give us the freedom to go in any direction. I found that very refreshing. He loved to put people together, step back and see what would happen. As a result a lot of us grew and learned a lot about ourselves."

The team ministry "was rocky in the sense that the sisters didn't know how to be on the pastoral teams any more than the priests knew how to work with them," concludes Sister Judy Warmbold. "It was trial by fire, it was experimentation, it was jumping in the water. But that's characteristic of John Sullivan and his approach to ministry. His approach is we're going to do it now, and the fallout comes later . . . The key was lay ministry development. The laity loved what was going on, because everything was hopping. In North Platte, it was like what we all had hoped would happen after Vatican II. The charismatic movement, schools, religious education, and the ministry to the sick and the elderly — all of those ministries were just given these huge doses of energy. They had leaders and they were recruiting all these laypeople to serve. To this day, many of those lay leaders are still in North Platte."

The bottom line for John was that team ministry was consistent with his conviction that all Catholics — ordained and non-ordained — have a responsibility for building up the church and for service. It was consistent also with his belief that ministers must pay attention to each and every individual — the "anonymous people, faceless people," as he called them. He expressed these convictions both in a 1977 interview before he addressed the annual convocation of the National Federation of Priests' Councils, and in an August 1977 article in *Chicago Studies*, titled "The Common Responsibility of Believers."

Defining ministry

In the interview, John defined ministry as the right and responsibility of every adult believer, ordained or non-ordained — a theme that he would echo with frequency during his tenure as bishop both in Grand Island and Kansas City-St. Joseph. "Ministry is serving the genuine needs of others with a love that has its origin in faith and in the Lord," he said. "I have often said that I judge the health of a parish by trying to determine just how sensitive the members of that faith community are to the needs of one another and others outside the community and how they minister to or serve those needs. This is the acid test. Service or ministry is the activity that identifies a person of faith."

Additionally, John re-emphasized the goals of the team ministry: to provide a witness of Christian faith and love to the people of the diocese, both Catholic and non-Catholic; to build community on the parish and diocesan levels, bringing the people and their ministers together so that they can support one another in the faith, and especially in religious education; and to provide service to people on a personal, one-to-one basis.

In the *Chicago Studies* article, John wrote that a church that leans so heavily on the clergy alone must now become a church relying much more on the common responsibility of believers. "This is required on dogmatic grounds and not merely as a pastoral necessity. Even if we had a surplus of clergy, a surplus of religious, this still must be the case. The most common error among Catholics is the belief that the church is identified with the clergy, who are looked upon as being exclusively responsible for the church, or responsible only to God really. This dichotomy between priesthood and laity is no longer valid for thinking about ministry."

Crises of faith

He stressed also that people cannot have a mature commitment to the church unless they go through crises of faith. "The person who is going through such crises does not need apologetics," John wrote. "He does not need arguments, or documentation, or proof. What he needs more than anything else is to know another believer whom he knows is not a phony! . . . To encounter such a person is just one of the reasons why people have to be known. . . . After all, there are only two things that last. People are eternal, and essentially so are the relationships that exist between people . . . What we have given our lives to is people and the relationships that exist between people. I do not know how this can be realized unless we have smaller communities. And we have the reverse."

Throughout his tenure as bishop, John continued to insist that there must be pastoral institutes to equip people for ministry. "I always dreamed of having a center for lay ministry in Grand Island," he recalls. "Maureen (Kelly) and I presented this idea to the priests, that we would have a summer institute (in 1977). Many of the priests called it my 'Louvain of the Plains.' Archbishop May, even back in the Extension days, had always called it 'the shimmering mirage.'" Adds Sister Regina McCarthy, "The diocesan byline of the Sullivan days was Bishop Sullivan wants a 'Louvain of the Plains.' He tried to make that happen and our clergy just wasn't ready for it."

In August 1975, John described the institute as a diocesan facility to train sisters, priests and laity in Scripture, catechetics, liturgy, and other topics. The institute could be staffed by the best qualified people in the country and could be utilized by neighboring dioceses. "Such institutes will be springing up around the country soon, but we should pioneer in this for the sake of our people," he noted. He acknowledged in 1976 that some of the obstacles were funds, the lack of conviction as to the urgent necessity of such an institute and that such an investment was the proper strategy or solution to the problem of perfecting ministry skills.

John concluded in the *Chicago Studies* article: "Fifteen years ago there were nearly 500 seminaries in this country, religious, diocesan, minor, major; there were 75 in one state alone. If we could afford to maintain 500 seminaries, certainly we could start with one or two institutes where we could have a concentration of people in the best of these fields who could reproduce themselves, who could really equip people to minister. We are often presumptuous and we procrastinate. Procrastination and half measures are . . . the great problems."

A diocesan woman

One measure John considered seriously during the 1970s was the idea of a "diocesan woman" who would commit herself to a particular diocese for ministry and become part of that diocese on a semi-permanent basis. "What I was interested in was a woman who would not be employed but be incardinated like a diocesan priest," he recalls. "For years, the women's communities were practicing the evangelical counsels. Their services meant the church could provide all kinds of religious education and health care. What I was exploring was why there couldn't be a diocesan woman who made a professional salary. And there would be this continued pursuit of the spirit of the counsels. I discussed the wisdom of this idea with many people all over the country informally, but never took any steps to pursue the concept. The idea frightened so many people because it was not really too far away from the ordination of women."

John outlined this idea in an April 1974 talk on the religious woman of the future. "She will be a very pastoral person in any one of several different possible capacities and will not simply be relieving a priest in his work," he said. "But rather she will bring her own special witness and strengths and talents that no one else can provide to serve people . . . She will probably in most cases commit herself to a particular diocese or geographic area and really become part of that diocese on a 12-month basis. The diocese, on the other hand, will incur a responsibility toward her similar to its responsibility toward diocesan priests . . . The great differences between the religious women of the past and those in the future would include their relationship to the diocese whereby they truly become part of the pastoral planning of that particular place and a vital part of the strategy."

With many regrets

It was "with many regrets" that John said goodbye to the people in the diocese of Grand Island upon the announcement by Pope Paul VI on June 27, 1977 that he was to succeed retiring Bishop Charles H. Helmsing as head of the Diocese of Kansas City-St. Joseph, Missouri. Bishop Helmsing had submitted his resignation in November 1976 because of failing health. John would turn 57 on July 5. "It is with considerable fear and trembling that I anticipate trying to succeed Bishop Helmsing," John said in a statement to the people of Kansas City-St. Joseph. "For many years, I have admired him as a priest and a bishop. It is so typical of him, in his very special concern for people, to resign the rather burdensome office of bishop of the diocese at the first sign of poor health. That song from the play, 'Oklahoma!', relates that 'everything is up to date in Kansas City,' and that is due in great part to Bishop Helmsing's leadership, but as I look forward to this new challenge, I hope 'they haven't gone as far as they can go.'"

John's tenure in Grand Island was marked by his goal to be a very pastoral bishop who tried to know as many people personally as he could, concludes Father Bernard Berger. Adds Sister Judy Warmbold: "His gift to Grand Island was timely and good. Serving with him was a revolutionary experience in my life — it changed the course of my life in terms of ministry. If you asked him, he'd probably say there was much he wasn't able to accomplish. He always felt the lay ministry development was not enough. But what he did accomplish was a good start. And that was recognized and he was moved to a bigger arena."

Perhaps John's own assessment of his service, of the role of the bishop as facilitator of ministry, came in his *Chicago Studies* article, published as he was being transferred to Kansas City-St. Joseph. "Bishops really do have to be the facilitator but they must not push too much," he wrote. "They also have to have patience . . . Even if a diocese were saturated with priests and sisters, the ministerial responsibility of our people would still be valid. Needs change, but for years we directed all our attention, energies and resources in one direction. We need to have the flexibility to change, to respond to where the needs are present. People often say that they can't wait until the dust settles. Well, the dust is not going to settle. We have to be prepared to change our view of ministry again as the needs indicate. People want me to give them a job definition. The job definition is the needs of the people."

CHAPTER SIX

Diocese of Kansas City-St. Joseph: The Early Years

JOHN'S FIRST TRIP TO KANSAS CITY CAME FOR THE OCCASION OF a press conference on July 1, 1977. During the press conference, John showed his love for people. His eyes filled with tears when he talked about the hard part of his transfer from Grand Island — leaving the priests, sisters and others whom he considered family.

He also displayed his sense of humor. Asked how he felt about coming to Kansas City, he told *The Kansas City Times*, "Bishop Helmsing is going to give me a lot of help. He's even going to tell me who his barber is," to which the balding Bishop Helmsing laughed heartily and responded, "I cut my own hair." John, feigning worry, said, "When he came here, he had a full head of hair."

In an interview with *The Kansas City Times*, John expressed these views on several issues confronting the church:

- On the bishop's availability: "I want to spend my time out in the field. I know there is a certain amount of administrative work, but I want to meet the people."

- On the lifestyle of a bishop: "A bishop cannot abandon his responsibilities, but I feel that someone coming into the diocese and seeing a group of priests together shouldn't be able to tell which one was a bishop."

- On the role he intended to play in the parochial school system: "I plan to play a major role in support. There is no substitute for it. But I feel the schools are not just for the diocese. We must minister to the total population."

- On how the church should deal with divorced Catholics: "The laws haven't changed. The indissolubility of marriage is still there. But the procedures are much better. A great emphasis has to be put on the diocesan tribunal to solve as many of these cases as possible. Some people may be in impossible situations. But still the church can minister to them. The church can let them know that they are loved and that you're pulling for them."

- On married priests: "We won't see it in our lifetime. There is so much witness value in celibacy."

- On women's ordination to the priesthood: "Theologically the question has not been resolved. Women clergy would be a sociological problem today apart from the theological problem. . . . Women need to be in the mainstream of the diocese in planning and decision making. Sisters are full-time non-ordained ministers with a ministry of their own."

John then asked *The Times* reporter (Helen T. Gray) whether he had answered the last question fully. "Well, you didn't give me a yes or a no," the reporter said. "One time someone asked me what my favorite color was," John recalled, "and I said, 'plaid.'"

Strong pastoral sense

In a July 3 interview with the diocesan newspaper, *The Catholic Key*, John said the first requirement of the role of a modern bishop was a strong pastoral sense — an ability to identify the needs of the people. He cited also shared responsibility in planning and decision-making as marks of a post-Vatican II bishop. "A bishop must serve the total population," he said. "In Grand Island we have made quite a commitment to a variety of ministries, both ordained and non-ordained. We have divided some very large parishes and consolidated some of the very small ones, which did not have sufficient resources for strong community. The support in faith must come from community, and effective evangelization is so important for a strong faith community."

John indicated that the process of changing from one diocese to another was "awesome." "I have far more questions than answers," he noted. In comparison to Grand Island, the Diocese of Kansas City-St. Joseph covered an area of more than 15,000 square miles within 27 counties in Missouri. The total population was 1,271,000, of which 136,000 were Catholic. The diocese was served by 371 priests (diocesan and religious) and 605 sisters.

In a ceremony that was both stately and humbling, solemn and joyous, John was installed Aug. 17, 1977 as the fourth bishop of Kansas City-St. Joseph. About 1,300 persons filled the Cathedral of the Immaculate Conception in downtown Kansas City. Some 400 others watched the ceremony on monitors at the Catholic Formation Center next door. The impressive processional included two cardinals, more than 50 archbishops and bishops and more than 200 priests. Those attending heard the metropolitan of the four Missouri dioceses, Cardinal John Carberry, archbishop of St. Louis, speak warm words of appreciation for Bishop Helmsing and John. Bishop George K. Fitzsimons, auxiliary bishop of the diocese, read John's letter of appointment from the apostolic delegate to the United States, Archbishop Jean Jadot.

A calling to service

Addressing his new flock for the first time, John admitted that he was overwhelmed. He spoke of a calling to service — his and the people's. Tears came to his eyes and his voice quivered as he admitted the difficulty in responding to the call to Kansas City-St. Joseph because of the great affection he had developed for the people in the Diocese of Grand Island. He said, however, his hopes for his new calling were high, and he wanted to share them with the people of the diocese, whom he said also were called to a new beginning. "You all share this call, this responsibility with me," he said, "and I know you will be faithful to the call, that you will be a responsive and not an apathetic church."

John listed three aspects of this calling:

- Bear witness of the Good News. As he had emphasized in his installation homily in Grand Island, John said, "You and I have so much to say to the men and women of our time. Some of us do it by preaching, but all of us must do it by the witness of our lives."

- Foster unity. "We must make the unity for which Christ prayed a reality," he said. "We are called to bring Christ to the world by our witness and unity. He added that Catholics are called to unity with men and women of other faiths, "especially our Jewish brothers and sisters," and to all people, even those with no faith.

- Help others. "We are called to translate the love we profess into action," John said. "We are called, not to be the fortress church, but the servant church."

John also made it clear that his priority was people and that people must be the priority of those in the diocese. He stated that at the heart of loving people is paying attention to them, and he pointed out that Christ paid attention to people.

At a reception and dinner for 1,400 people at the Radisson Muehlebach Hotel following the installation Mass, Cardinal William Baum, archbishop of Washington and a priest of the Diocese of Kansas City-St. Joseph, noted John's great warmth and love for people. On the light side, he "warned" the diocesan priests that John had an amazing memory.

John, who was humorous in many of his remarks, said that life is like a mosaic. "And I think that every part of my mosaic is here tonight, including three high school girl friends." He said that his little niece recently asked him when the "insulation" was (referring to the installation). John said that question had a great deal of meaning for him because insulation comes from the word for island. "Bishops sometimes feel like islands," he said. "But no man is an island. So many of you have kept me from being an island, and I hope you won't permit me to be insulated. We're in this thing together."

A lot of energy

Father Patrick Rush, who was serving as vice chancellor and director of the permanent diaconate for the diocese when John became bishop, recalls that John "came in with a whole agenda and a whole lot of energy, and he hit the ground running with that agenda. He was a whole change of style from Bishop Helmsing. Whereas Bishop Helmsing was very interested in liturgical rubrics, very knowledgeable in theology and a master of group meetings, Bishop Sullivan was not an academician or a theologian. He was very pastoral, very outgoing, and had tremendous street smarts."

Father Rush adds, "Bishop Sullivan indicated pretty much from the beginning that he wanted to handle the assignment of priests personally, and that he was going to address some of the priest personnel issues that had been plaguing the diocese. Initially he also hosted a meeting of women religious superiors, trying to encourage their personnel to serve the diocese in new ways." That meeting took place Dec. 11, 1977, with 49 superiors of religious women working in the diocese. John described the meeting as "an opportunity for us to share our hopes and expectations for sisters in the future in the diocese."

Establishes center

Just five months after his installation, John announced that the diocese would establish the Center for Pastoral Ministry in Kansas City to begin operations in the fall of 1978. He also named Father William Bauman, pastor of St. Stephen's Parish and vicar for education, as director of the Center. The Center, he envisioned, would become the heart of pastoral, catechetical and ministerial growth and development within the diocese and the greater Midwest region. John's consultation in forming this plan included (in December 1977) the Vicariate for Education, the Diocesan Council of Women Religious, the Diocesan Pastoral Council and the Diocesan Senate of Priests (which unanimously endorsed the idea). In addition, Father Bauman and John convened a "think tank" of experts on Jan. 27-28 in Kansas City, including 11 resource persons and 22 local persons, to explore models of ministry education. Some of the national experts included Dolores Leckey, executive director of the National Conference of Catholic Bishops' Secretariat on the Laity, Bishop Albert Ottenweller of Steubenville, Ohio, and Auxiliary Bishop Daniel Hart of Boston, Massachusetts. Additional consultation was conducted with Father Dennis Geaney of the Catholic Theological Union in Chicago and Msgr. John Egan of the University of Notre Dame.

In making the announcement, John echoed a familiar message: "We have no one recognized center where some of the best teachers and experts within the United States can work together for the growth of pastoral ministry. We need a model. We need excellence. We need training for priests, sisters, and for the mother and father of four who want to serve well in their parishes." John said a particular emphasis would be placed on the many emerging forms of lay ministry. The structure of the Center's offerings would be twofold: to serve the full-time committed professional and to competently assist the layperson seeking to develop his or her talents and contribute significantly to the parish. Top priority was given to the selection of at least six of the best national experts to act as instructors within the fields of scripture, catechetics, ministry, doctrine, liturgy, pastoral skills, church history, evangelization, social justice and marriage and family life. At first, a significant part of the Center's courses and activity would be located in "pilot parishes" which would be spread throughout the diocese.

"This has been a dream of mine for eight to ten years," John said. "I'm delighted that what my friends in Grand Island had jokingly referred to as 'Sullivan's shimmering mirage' is now able to become a reality in Kansas City." John also indicated that the diocese had received a substantial donation from the Catholic Church Extension Society ($100,000 per year for several years) that would free up funds to make the Center possible without additional financial burdens.

Father Bauman remembers that much of the spring of 1978 was spent meeting with parish staffs, religious and lay persons in the various deaneries of the diocese "to sell the idea of the Center and process it so that people could accept it. I was also on the road trying to recruit the staff. It was an exciting project and it was putting an idea in place that many of us had believed in beforehand. Bishop Sullivan took something that was on the periphery and moved it to be the centerpiece." In all, Father Bauman presided over nine "town hall" parish meetings with an attendance of more than 540 people; 11 deanery meetings with priests; meetings with Conception Abbey, Rockhurst College and Avila College; and groups including youth ministers, religious education coordinators, high school faculties and the priests' continuing education board. A six-person task force helped him combine the data of these 700-plus persons into the Center's action plan. A staff of seven persons was hired.

Reaction a bit polarized

What was the reaction of the priests and laity? "Because the Center was moving with such strength and force, the reaction was a bit polarized," Father Bauman says.

"There were people who were not in favor of moving fast with change in the church, who would therefore cry out that there was not enough involvement and process. Then there were those who were very much in favor of this growth who saw it as the fulfillment of their dream. Then there were some diocesan people in ministry who saw their own previous involvements shrink into the background. So there were all the normal human forces at work.

"There was always this question of ownership about the Center," he adds. "There was later much criticism on this issue. As I look back on it, we did an awful lot of process, but we may have been so determined to succeed that even if we had slowed down the process we would have still plowed ahead."

John says that the greatest resistance to the Center came from the priests. "Some of the priests felt they didn't have sufficient ownership," he assesses. "But we had the unanimous support of the priests' senate. I feared that I had been too aggressive with the idea on my part and that made for some division. I do admit that it took several years for the Center to have the proper focus. Many in the diocese thought the staff would just come out to a parish at Advent or Lent to present some series or continuing education. But from the beginning, the whole idea was to provide training and formation for ministry, with a great emphasis on education in their faith. I've taken some flak about the Center over the years, but I just ignored much of it. I was determined that it was going to go. I knew I was right. I suppose it came from my whole history before I got to Kansas City."

Maureen Kelly, one of the Center's first staff members, recalls, "I never thought the lack of support was because John was a supporter of lay ministry, but because he might have been perceived as a bull in a china shop. Because the seeds of the idea had already blossomed in him before he got to Kansas City, it didn't dawn on him that everyone didn't think it was a good idea or that he had to get everyone on board first. Perhaps he didn't give the diocese and the people enough time to own the idea, so some of the priests felt disenfranchised."

Adds Father Rush, "Bishop Sullivan's vision always was, if we spend all this money on seminaries for education of priests . . . we've also got to start channeling funds and educate the laity. Having said that, it was very experimental as to how we do that and what it looks like. So the Center went through quite a metamorphosis over the years, trying to define formation and training and adult education." The priests' initial reaction, he says, may have been partially due to changing times and roles in the church.

The first classes offered by the Center began Oct. 1, 1978. These included 17 basic offerings in response to parish needs and plans developed during the planning sessions earlier in the year. The offerings included topics ranging from theology and spirituality to methods for religious education and basics in counseling. Catechist formation and training were also a high priority for the Center. (The Center's name was changed to the Center for Pastoral Life and Ministry in 1980.)

Other changes

During John's first full year as bishop he initiated other changes and activities. Early on, he showed his interest in placing more laypeople in diocesan administrative posts, says Joseph Connor, whom John promoted from assistant comptroller to comptroller in December 1977. "I was the first lay employee of the diocese really to assume any administrative responsibility," he remembers. "As a result, I was the first layperson to be named the treasurer of the diocesan corporation." At the same time, a concentrated evangelization program was initiated in four central city parishes, with the Rite of Christian Initiation of Adults begun in these parishes.

John indicated also he wanted a major shift in the delivery of services through the diocesan Catholic Charities agency, recalls Neal Colby, current director of Catholic Charities who was an associate director in 1977. John moved the agency from a leased building to a diocesan-owned building adjacent to the cathedral in downtown Kansas City. "This was my first insight that here was a person with definite opinions about what should be done in the diocese," Colby remembers. "At the first meeting of our board, he said he wanted services decentralized to the parish level. He felt people encounter Christ at the parish, so that's where our services should be located. He told us, 'I'm going to keep your feet to the fire until this is done.' After the meeting, he told me he hoped to see a social worker in every parish in the diocese. I went a little dizzy, because we had maybe six social workers on staff and almost 100 parishes. It seemed like the 'loaves and fishes' story to me."

Colby adds, "My first impressions of him were very vivid and somewhat confusing and challenging. These initial impressions were symbolic of Bishop Sullivan's relationship with me, the agency and the diocese as a whole, in the sense that he had a vision of church that was very broad, challenging and to some extent, very revolutionary, although it certainly fit with Vatican II. He saw, I think, the finished edifice from a distance and he could describe it in pretty good detail. What served to be the challenge, however, for those of us who worked for him, was how to get from here to there."

No preferential treatment

The diocesan priest changes made by John in June 1978, particularly the reassignment of Msgr. Vincent L. Kearney from Christ the King Parish in south Kansas City (after 22 years as pastor), caused major controversy and attracted national attention. The pastoral changes were perhaps not so much a showdown between conservatives and liberals or a flexing of administrative authority as they were a signal of the beginning of the end of any semblance of preferential treatment among diocesan priests. Msgr. Kearney's was one of 42 priest changes announced at the time, the most extensive shifting of parish priests in the diocese's recent history.

"One of the first obstacles in my way as bishop was that seven of the priests resisted any transfer to another parish. And some of them were my seminary schoolmates, including Msgr. Kearney," John recalls. "But I had to make changes. One priest had come in to see me who was a very earnest, hard-working man, not identified with any particular group, right or left. He said 'why should I move when some of the others won't?' He called these seven priests 'the untouchables.' So I realized in all justice that I had to confront this problem. One priest had been 29 years in the same parish, another one 22 years." When someone warned John that he would rise or fall on this issue, he replied, "I didn't come here to rise or fall, but to do God's will."

When word first leaked out about the change of Msgr. Kearney from Christ the King, John remembers that all the mail was attacking him. Later it ran about 40 to 60% in favor. Many parishioners of Christ the King were upset when they learned their pastor would be moved. For many years, the parish had attracted Catholics who favored the pre-Vatican II liturgical orientation of the church and who opposed many of the Council's changes. But despite the negative mail, the phone calls, a protest march on the diocesan chancery and the publicity, John told *The Kansas City Times* in an interview published June 13, 1978 that if he had to do it over again, he would make the same decision.

"I could not move any reluctant pastors — and every good parish priest is reluctant to leave the people he loves and serves — as long as there are some priests who absolutely refuse to move," he said. "In other words, you can't make exceptions when you have any preferential people who can't be moved. If men who have been in parishes for an unusually extended period are not moved, then every other priest in this diocese could refuse to move. If you want to kill morale in a diocese, one way to do it is to have a situation where the priests are not treated equally."

In *The Kansas City Times* interview, John said he was not in favor of every priest being moved at a set time, but he was in favor of transfers within a reasonable time period. John had begun meeting with the priests' personnel board of the diocese in the fall of 1977. They had gone over every parish and every priest to assess what man would be best suited for what parish. John had by this time visited the large majority of parishes and had talked to almost every priest. He believed that if he was going to make any major moves, he would have to do it early in his administration before any strong personal attachments developed. He also believed that coming from outside the diocese gave him a broader perspective of what was needed for the good of the entire diocese.

Paid heavily for his decision

"I feel I'll have to pay heavily for my decision," John told *The Times*. "People will wonder about me. But someone had to do this. I spent a lot of time with my head in my hands in the chapel. I can't tell you how many hours we have worked on this." John said he was not surprised that there had been a strong negative reaction, but was surprised by "the degree of obstinacy of some. I expected it. I didn't undertake these changes thinking all would be great." He saw his decision as a turning point in the diocese. John recalled how he felt when he received the letter informing him that he was being transferred from Grand Island. "I didn't want to move," he said. "I grieved for about two hours after I got the letter. But I moved because I made a vow to be obedient."

Bishop Fitzsimons (now bishop of Salina, Kansas) was named by John to replace Msgr. Kearney as pastor of Christ the King. The negative reaction to the pastoral changes "hurt him (John) very much, because he's such a sensitive person," Bishop Fitzsimons recalls. "But he wanted to be true to his vision of church and the idea of involving more people in the life of the church."

Msgr. Kearney's views were publicized in a lengthy interview with Tom Leathers, editor of *The Squire*, a weekly newspaper published in Leawood, Kansas. The interview was reprinted in the conservative Catholic weekly, *The Wanderer*, on August 3, 1978. Msgr. Kearney appealed his transfer to Vatican authorities, and eventually Archbishop Thomas A. Donnellan of Atlanta was appointed in the early 1980s as apostolic visitator on the case. Msgr. Kearney eventually agreed to withdraw his protest. According to an agreement signed in May 1983 by Msgr. Kearney, John, Msgr. Robert Hogan (diocesan chancellor) and Archbishop Donnellan, Msgr. Kearney retired, but continued to celebrate Mass in his suburban Kansas home.

"The whole incident surprised Bishop Sullivan," says Father Richard Carney, a canon lawyer, who in 1978 was director of the diocesan marriage tribunal and has been diocesan chancellor since 1986. "Kearney just turned him down flat and I think that jolted him. I think he expected Kearney to move. And then he didn't know the whole thing was going to come down to a battle, and he didn't want that because he's not a battler, he doesn't like fights. But the truth is Bishop Sullivan did nothing to cause the canonical fight he finally had to get into. . . . Kearney instigated the activity and involvement of Rome."

An awesome responsibility

Father Gerald Waris, now pastor of St. Peter's Parish in Kansas City, was on the priests' personnel board when the controversial changes were made. "We all knew what an awesome responsibility Bishop Sullivan had in the whole aspect of priest personnel," he remembers. "We knew that it was going to be a challenge and a difficult task for him. I saw the agony in his heart in facing these problems. And the personnel board could see it. . . . That's what spurred the personnel board and encouraged us to make the necessary moves. But Bishop Sullivan took the flak for it. It caused him a lot of grief. He didn't take any personal satisfaction in making the moves."

John's behavior was an example of "grace under pressure," contends Father John Schuele, who had been a priest only about two years at the time of the changes. "Bishop Sullivan was slandered in *The Squire* article . . . not only did he not correct the article, nor reply to the falsehoods, he never made a public statement against his adversaries. To this day, that still seems incredible to me. It showed me what kind of person he was."

Following the priest changes, conservative Catholics in the diocese continued to clash with John, including the filing of lawsuits against the diocese. The clashes at some parishes, notably Christ the King and St. Catherine's, were linked with the reality that the "immovable" pastors had resisted or failed to implement much of the Vatican II renewal of the liturgy. In late 1978, some 70 members of Christ the King sued the diocese to try to obtain detailed information on diocesan finances. Although a Jackson County judge ruled in 1980 in favor of the diocese, the challenge was virtually unprecedented at the time. In 1980, a Jackson County judge ruled that parishioners of St. Catherine's, upset over the removal of a communion rail, did not have a property right to it. That same year, the diocese unknowingly sold (through an intermediary) the former St. Vincent de Paul church building to local traditionalist followers of French Archbishop Marcel Lefebvre, suspended by the Vatican in 1975 for his refusal to adhere to Vatican II reforms.

In late April 1981, diocesan officials (including Bishop Fitzsimons) had to seal the church doors at Christ the King and hire off-duty police officers to guard them, to keep out parishioners protesting the moving of the tabernacle from the altar to a specially constructed pedestal 15 feet away. The diocese was granted a temporary restraining order to keep at least nine persons from interfering with the construction.

May defends actions

Throughout these controversies, John's close friend, Archbishop John May of St. Louis, consistently defended his actions, especially after articles by Frank Morriss criticizing John appeared in February 1981 in *The Wanderer*. In a letter to his priests, Archbishop May noted, "Again and again I have seen some of the most faithful and devoted bishops in this country undermined in this way and their dioceses scandalized by such hateful diatribes. Knowing the facts in this case as I do, I do not feel justified in keeping silence." In a letter published in *The Wanderer* on April 16, 1981, Archbishop May wrote, "People of all faiths in the Kansas City area have been scandalized by these years of vituperation by this small group of Catholics against their bishop, a man who has the love and loyalty of the vast majority of the clergy and laity of the diocese not to mention the support of the pope and his brother bishops. Your articles gave national approval to this local scandal and so I protested."

Vision for the diocese

Perhaps the most significant event of John's early years in Kansas City-St. Joseph was his "Vision for the Diocese" presented on Nov. 24, 1980. More than 350 ministerial leaders from throughout the diocese gathered to hear John emphasize the parish as the primary faith community. He outlined his views for the future and spelled out specific goals. The thrust of his statement was consistent with his approach to ministry over the years: he believed his vision could be actualized because he recognized the unique ministry of the church.

"Ultimately, my belief in the attainability of these dreams and goals stems from our shared faith," John said. "We need continually to remind ourselves that the church is not a mere human enterprise, but a mystery. . . . We cannot think of the church as an institution, a human corporation, into which we infuse the abstraction of mystery. For us, the church is real — it is a real, historic, happening-in-this-day, a happening-in-this-hall event. It is a compendium of relations and interactions which, for most of us, are manifested primarily in parish communities."

As he had done when establishing the Center for Pastoral Ministry, John emphasized that ministry is not a function of delegation but a function of one's baptism. "My vision for the church of Kansas City-St. Joseph is one in which faith-filled and competent ministers will serve and one in which the diocese is covered with healthy, prospering faith communities," he stated. "I dream of the day (and I don't believe it is far off) when we will have very complete data and professional expertise in planning, and can aggressively pursue recruiting full-time religious and lay staff members to provide a total ministry for our parishes."

Among the specific goals John cited were: that by 1984 every parish will have participated in a planning effort, including a formal needs assessment of the community and priorities; that the catechumenate would have a central role and be the principal thrust not only for evangelization but also for parish renewal; that religious education programs be improved and expanded; and that efforts in inner city and rural ministries be expanded.

"During the past 39 months I've focused my major efforts in three areas: the reduction of the diocesan debt to a 'manageable' level; the establishment of the Center for Pastoral Ministry as a resource for parish renewal; and the elimination of what I perceived to be — and what others advised me to be — 'islands' of dissension which were ultimately harmful to the unity of our church," John concluded. "All of these are things I felt were necessary prerequisites for any authentic diocesan renewal program. There have been more than a few moments during this time when I encountered frustration and negativism. There have been some discouraging events of which I'm sure you are all aware. But there have been many, many more moments of joy, of sharing, of optimism and of sincere, honest affection. . . . I have only limited faith in 'my' vision: I have limitless belief in 'our' vision."

Repays diocesan debt

While John was well-known for his keen pastoral sense as a bishop, less known was his head for figures and his insistence on balanced budgets. From his arrival in Kansas City-St. Joseph, he made repayment of the diocesan debt of $6.7 million one of his earliest and highest priorities. "We had this inability to expand," he says. "We were paying this horrendous interest. And not only interest, but then demand payments on the principal, which were heavy. We had to make so many demands on the parishes in order to meet our diocesan debt that they were limited." The debt had been incurred during a period of almost 20 years, beginning shortly after the combining of the dioceses of Kansas City and St. Joseph in 1956. Capital improvements to diocesan high schools, St. John's high school seminary, diocesan Newman Centers, some operating deficits of various diocesan services, and acquisition of property as potential parish sites formed the bulk of the debt.

John charted a three-point attack. In an austerity move, he consolidated several chancery departments and administrative offices to provide better service; he directed that consideration be given to the sale of any tract of real estate not essential for the mission of the church; and he asked for increased support for the annual United Catholic Appeal. On August 17, 1984, the seventh anniversary of John's installation as bishop, the diocese made the final payment of $518,751 on its debt. With the retirement of the debt, John noted that the diocese must turn its attention to other needs, such as additional funding and more stability for retirement plans for priests and lay employees.

Diocesan comptroller Joseph Connor, who worked most closely with John in eliminating the debt, notes that "Bishop Sullivan was certain and very sensitive that whatever he did he wanted to do it in a positive way. He did not want to reflect negatively on his predecessor, Bishop Helmsing, as far as the debt was concerned, since most of it was incurred before Bishop Helmsing came on the scene. Bishop Sullivan was always cautious and prudent when it came to finances. Whenever there were two or three options available to him, he always chose the highest road possible . . . today the pension plans for priests and lay people are very well-funded." Adds Father William Bauman, "Bishop Sullivan understood the debt problem. He uncovered how much the diocese had borrowed and took charge. He kept the goal in focus and pursued it relentlessly."

Appoints finance council

Connor notes that John also appointed a diocesan finance council (before it was required in the revised Code of Canon Law in 1983) to advise him. "Bishop Sullivan never had a closed-door attitude. Our role was always to listen and advise, and the bishop had the ultimate decision," says Joseph McGee, a member of the council since its inception. "We would all watch Bishop Sullivan agonize over the tough decisions. He never made an unpopular decision without prayerful consideration. He is such a compassionate person, yet he knew he couldn't say yes to everyone. It wasn't easy for him to say no when he had to. He brought the United Catholic (Stewardship) Appeal up considerably over the years. Having been a pastor for so long, he knew firsthand the financial problems of parishes. He always took a balanced approach. He knew he couldn't neglect the parishes because we had to ensure financial stability together."

During John's first seven years in the diocese, other efforts he initiated which stand out significantly include:

- A continual planning effort was initiated in the city of St. Joseph in 1979 to investigate needs and problems among its seven parishes. On Sept. 6, 1981, the first new parish in St. Joseph in more than 70 years was established, called for by the St. Joseph Planning Commission. The new church was completed and dedicated by John on Sept. 16, 1984. A diocesan office for pastoral planning was first established in February 1981. Also in 1981, ten parishes in the heart of Kansas City began participating in an inter-parish planning project. This culminated in nine of the parishes forming the Catholic Covenant Communities on March 15, 1984 to collaborate in ministries, foster solidarity among the parishes, and raise the visibility of the church in the wider community.

- A new diocesan policy for teenagers receiving the sacrament of Confirmation was announced May 28, 1982. Under the new guidelines, the sacrament was offered to candidates who had entered their sophomore year in high school. The 18-month program required 20-30 hours of community service along with the usual hours of instruction.

- The first collection of the Bishop's Emergency Assistance Fund was taken up in parishes on Feb. 28, 1982. John, in conjunction with the priests' senate in January 1982, had pledged to raise $100,000 to aid parishes in their assistance programs. All monies donated were used directly to aid the poor.

- Citing declining enrollment and an accompanying concern for proper stewardship of diocesan resources, John announced June 26, 1983 that St. John's High School Seminary would close. The decision came after meetings with parents and students of the seminary, diocesan priests, and representatives of the Vincentian Fathers who staffed the school. A diocesan youth retreat facility had already been operating out of the complex since November 1981, using the income from the proceeds of the sale of a diocesan youth camp in 1980. In subsequent years, St. John's was remodeled to serve as a center for diocesan activities.

- An estimated 4,500 persons gathered Sept. 9-10, 1983 for the diocesan ministry convention, representing nearly all the parishes. At the closing Mass, John noted in his homily, "All of us here have witnessed the richness of ministries active in our diocese. We have met so many people who live ministry in their daily lives. . . . As bishop I have a very simple vision for the Diocese of Kansas City-St. Joseph: that every person who lives within it will have, at some point in his or her life, exposure to the affection, the witness and the support of the Catholic Christian believer. In essence, that's what I've been about during these past six years. . . . We have been outlining what we judge to be the specific challenges facing our diocese at this point in time: the challenges of fostering lay ministry, of allocation and management of resources, and of a renewed understanding of the role of the ordained minister in today's church."

- The Emmaus spirituality program in 1983-1984 was designed to offer spiritual renewal to the priests of the diocese. The 12-month program, with a focus on Scripture and prayer, involved over 90% of the priests in the diocese, including John, Bishop Helmsing and Bishop Fitzsimons. After two retreats and six overnight small group meetings, the program ended with a presbyterial convention on June 4-5, 1984.

"Being a priest in 1983 one finds oneself caught in a crossfire of contradictory expectations," John told diocesan priests as the Emmaus program began. "On the one side, a significant number of parishioners demand the priest assume a customary traditional role as the ultimate leader of all parish community activities. . . . On the other hand, a growing number of laity are asking for and assuming the responsibility for key parish ministries . . . the need for a renewed understanding of the role of the ordained minister is crucial."

First ad limina visit

In December 1983, John and Msgr. Robert Hogan, his close friend and diocesan chancellor, traveled to the Vatican to meet with Pope John Paul II for his first "ad limina" visit as ordinary of Kansas City-St. Joseph. It was his lot to make his debut after the release of two Vatican documents — announcing inquiries into American seminaries and religious communities of priests, sisters and brothers — caused concern among some in the American Catholic community. Before he left for Rome, John in October 1983 held three listening sessions with 33 religious communities serving in the diocese, representing 756 priests, brothers and sisters.

A *Kansas City Star* feature article on John published Dec. 4, 1983 characterized him politically as somewhere between then-Archbishop Raymond Hunthausen of Seattle, a prominent critic of nuclear arms, and the majority of American bishops, who approved a May 1983 pastoral letter demanding an end to the nuclear arms race.

"He's well-integrated as a human being," Eugene Kennedy, a psychologist with Loyola University in Chicago, told *The Star*. Kennedy, who prepared a psychological study of priests for the U.S. bishops in 1971, added, "He (John) doesn't say one thing and mean another. He's healthy. When you have one who seems to mean what he says — and there seems to be no difference between the public person and the private person — that's what I mean by healthy. That's what I believe your bishop (John) is. It makes him exceptional."

CHAPTER SEVEN

Diocese of Kansas City-St. Joseph: The Later Years

"THE DYNAMIC OF FAITH COMPELS LOVE; IT COMPELS ACTION; IT compels a thirst and a concern for the well-being of others and for justice." This passage from John's "Vision" statement of 1980 aptly characterizes a primary thrust of his tenure in Kansas City-St. Joseph, especially in his later years of service. His concern for social justice, for rural people, for minority groups and for the poor was exemplified through many programs, including the establishment of the Central City School Fund, the parish-based ministry plan, and a "partnership with parishes" emphasis within Catholic Charities.

"The poor in Kansas City are a priority," John told *Kansas City Magazine* in May 1986. "The church has to be in the inner city or we might as well close up." Although the diocese at the time had no cash surplus, he allocated much of the diocesan budget for services in the inner city, including more than 50 emergency centers. The actual Catholic population in the inner city was low, but the diocese spent nearly $1 million annually to subsidize central city Catholic primary schools and four diocesan high schools. John noted also that he had placed some of his most dynamic young priests at the helm of inner city churches where they were actively involved in the rehabilitation of their communities. "Putting vital men in the inner city is a signal to the rest of the faithful," he said.

One of those priests, Father Michael Roach, who served as pastor of the Church of the Risen Christ in Kansas City during the 1980s, says that it was John's personal style "that made those in the inner city, especially African-American Catholics, feel a great affection for him. His caring for the parishes and his personability went very far. People knew where his heart was. He wanted to meet them where they were, whether it was addressing the needs of kids' self esteem, African-American culture or single-parent families." As John noted in a talk to diocesan African-American Catholics preparing for a National Black Catholic Congress in November 1986, the church "has a history of some successes but far too many failures in either educating or evangelizing the black community specifically . . . We must develop a greater awareness of the need for education and evangelization."

Confronts social issues

John's willingness to confront social issues came concurrently with the U.S. bishops issuing a controversial pastoral letter on war and peace in 1983, which questioned the build-up of nuclear arms, and the 1986 pastoral, "Economic Justice for All," which expressed indignation at the chasm between the rich and the poor. On his return from the U.S. bishops' meeting in November 1986, following the approval of the economic pastoral, John called it a "historic document" which called Catholics to a conversion process examining their own sense of values. That same fall, John addressed the concerns of rural families facing economic hardships in a pastoral statement and a series of "Town and Country" days across the diocese. "As the people of God, we are called to care for those who suffer, search with them for justice, and speak to them the word of hope," he said. "There are new opportunities for dialogue between members of rural communities, between public decision-makers and people affected by those decisions. We, the people of God who share God's vision of

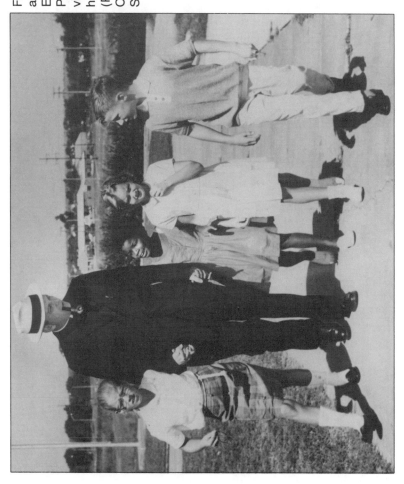

Father John J. Sullivan, as director of the
Extension Lay Volunteer Program during the 1960s, visited with children in the home missions. (Photo courtesy of the Catholic Church Extension Society)

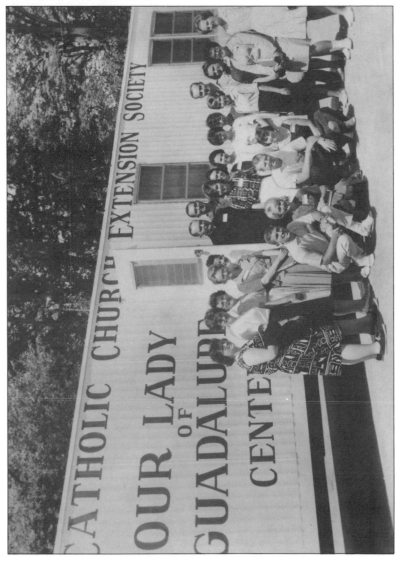

Father Sullivan visits some of the Extension Lay Volunteers (Photo courtesy of the Catholic Church Extension Society)

Bishop Sullivan greets some Sisters of Mercy
at groundbreaking ceremonies at St. Mary's High School
in Independence, Missouri, in 1987.

Bishop Sullivan visits with seminarians of the Diocese
of Kansas City-St. Joseph during a picnic in 1977.

Just before installation ceremonies in Kansas City on August 17,
1977, Bishop John Sullivan (center) poses with (left to right)
Cardinal William Baum, Bishop Charles Helmsing,
Archbishop Jean Jadot (apostolic delegate)
and retired Bishop John Paschang of Grand Island.

Bishop Sullivan in this 1987 photo chats with his two close
advisors during his tenure in Kansas City-St. Joseph. From left:
Father Richard Carney, diocesan chancellor,
Father Norman Rotert, vicar general, and Bishop Sullivan.

Bishop Sullivan (right) and Archbishop John May of St. Louis (center) visit with Father Michael Coleman of the marriage tribunal in Kansas City, 1987.

Bishop Sullivan discusses ministry efforts in 1987 with George Noonan, director of the Center for Pastoral Life and Ministry, centered in Kansas City.

In his study in his home in Kansas City, Bishop Sullivan prepares a homily in 1987.

Bishop Sullivan shows photos of the parishes he served to Julie Sly, editor of *The Catholic Key*, on his 10th anniversary as bishop of the diocese.

Bishop Sullivan speaks with Scott Francis Families Foundation and John Palmer, Board member of the Central City School Fund, during the Sept. 3 Donor Appreciation luncheon, 1992.

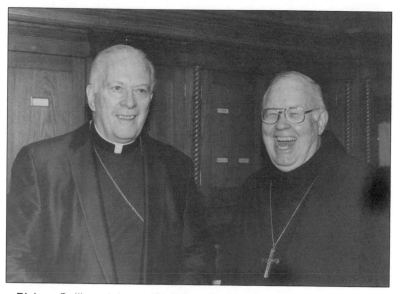

Bishop Sullivan jokes with Abbot James Jones, former abbot of Conception Abbey in Conception, Missouri.

People of the Diocese of Kansas City-St. Joseph gather around Bishop Sullivan during a retirement celebration at the Cathedral of the Immaculate Conception in August, 1993.

Bishop Sullivan is delighted with the presence of children during the dedication of a preschool in his name in northeast Kansas City.

justice and community, must be an active agent of hope, exploring meaningful dialogue wherever possible."

Throughout the 1980s and early 1990s, John effectively raised the consciousness of the entire diocesan community, Catholic and non-Catholic, around concern for the poor, says Father Norman Rotert, who served as John's vicar general from 1984 until his retirement in 1993. "He invited the larger community to share with us in the education of poor children through participation in the central city schools. He gave strong support to the work of organizing poor communities to help themselves. He assigned talented young priests to the inner city and was willing to sacrifice some other things in order for that to happen."

"There was never any question that Bishop Sullivan's heart was with the poor, and he was deeply committed," adds George Noonan, director of the diocesan Center for Pastoral Life and Ministry since 1984. "He genuinely believes that education is a way out of poverty. He believes that what Catholicism has to offer is a real way out. And the commitment is there in the sense of providing social services. It always bothered him that people ran to the suburbs to get away from problems instead of confronting them."

Parish ownership

Neal Colby, director of Catholic Charities since 1981, said that at John's urging the agency shifted to a "partnership with parishes" emphasis during the 1980s. "His vision for Catholic Charities was that it was our job to inspire and enable the parishes to run their own programs, if possible," Colby assesses. "This meant services to the elderly, emergency services, counseling, day care, housing, services to rural families and peace and justice advocacy. He always felt there needed to be parish ownership and control of social ministry. In retrospect, his intuitive sense was right that all of those programs were enhanced by developing this relationship." Colby also helped to design and implement a parish-based ministry program where diocesan grants were given to needy parishes for staff and ministerial programs. In 1987, the third year of the plan, 20 projects received some $214,000 in grants.

The diocesan peace and justice office took on a similar parish emphasis, says Christian Brother Michael Fehren-bach, who served as its director during the 1980s. "We constantly tried to create efforts that would exist at the parish level, rather than big diocesan programs," he says. "We tried to stay away from telling parishes what to do, but to provide training programs for what they wanted to do." John's "ad limina" report to Pope John Paul II for the years 1983-87 noted that the peace and justice office had extended its services to 54 parishes. Three parishes had begun a "twinning program" in which parishioners visited and supported parish communities in El Salvador, Guatemala or Nicaragua.

That same "ad limina" report noted that from 1983 to 1987, enrollment in Catholic schools in the diocese declined from 14,660 to 13,693 students. In 1987-88, 22% of the students in diocesan schools were from minority ethnic groups, while 24% were non-Catholic. Because some of the schools in the inner city had started to deteriorate financially, John worked on a way to save them. He began by meeting with people from the business community to see if they would be willing to form a partnership with the diocese to subsidize the central city Catholic schools in Kansas City. Out of those meetings, the Central City School Fund was established in 1988. John pledged $800,000 from the diocese to help maintain the central city schools. The diocese then looked to the community to match its financial contribution. A board of directors was appointed in 1989 to consult on the future directions and to help solicit contributions from the business community.

Simple conviction

"The simple conviction I kept sharing with people was that the only way out of poverty for these youngsters is education," John says. "I was always very optimistic about this and I still am. We had to put our money and give specialized attention to the inner city schools if they were going to survive. These schools are the best hope for many to break the cycles of educational illiteracy, economic poverty and moral impoverishment . . . the very last hope for some."

Sister Vickie Perkins, a member of the Sisters of Charity of Leavenworth and John's superintendent of diocesan schools, said that before the Central City School Fund was established, the parishes could not support the schools on their own. Tuition also was getting too high for many of the families in the inner city to afford. "What was going to happen if we didn't do something, was one by one the central city schools would close," she recalls. "And Bishop Sullivan knew the diocese couldn't continue subsidizing all of them. Some people were saying to him, 'Don't do this, it won't work.' But he finally said, 'We're going to do it.' It was his willing to risk that made it all happen."

The reaction has been extremely positive, Sister Vickie notes. "People have really seen that this is not just a Catholic issue because we can impact the lives of many poor children in this way. People have helped in many ways and not just financially. Part of that was due to the respect they had for Bishop Sullivan."

After the Central City School Fund was established, the next step was to restructure the schools to make the best use of the facilities available. The consolidation process began when principals and pastors met with school office personnel to examine the central city schools. They found declining enrollment and uncertain financing possibilities. The first restructuring began in 1989 when four small central city schools were consolidated to create St. Monica's School on two campuses. The new school served students living in the boundaries of seven Covenant Community parishes. The next year, St. John's School was merged with Holy Cross in northeast Kansas City and, in 1992, Our Lady of the Americas, Guardian Angels and Redemptorist Schools on the west side were merged to form Our Lady of the Angels and Our Lady of Guadalupe.

Helped schools financially

The restructuring helped secure the schools financially, Sister Vickie says. "The restructuring, coupled with raising the funds for the central city schools, created what Bishop Sullivan was dreaming of — a set of schools that will serve these children for years to come." She adds, "When Bishop Sullivan came here from Grand Island, the perception was that he did not support Catholic schools. But any of us who worked closely with him knew this was a very false perception. He knew Catholic schools were an extremely important ministry of the church, but they should never be the only ministry." By John's retirement in 1993, some 2,000 students were enrolled in the central city schools, with 48% of them living below the poverty level, 48% of them African-American, 25% Caucasian and 24% Hispanic. Some 46% of the students attending the schools were not Catholic, and the dropout rate was less than 3%. During 1992-93, the Central City School Fund contributed $1,442,590 to the schools.

Just as John realized planning and restructuring must take place in the schools to meet changing needs, so must such planning take place in regard to the diocese's parishes and their staffs. In July 1986, John placed a planning process in the hands of the people of the diocese by appointing a diocesan planning committee, consisting of 14 people assigned 14 different coordinating tasks. This committee broke into three task forces involving 50 people from across the diocese, addressing the issues of personnel, schools and finance. They held meetings for more than two years throughout the diocese, collecting and processing data from the parishes and deaneries. Each parish's role was to perform a self-study involving parishioners and staff, with the aid of a "Framework for Parish Planning" published and presented at a diocesan convocation on Nov. 15, 1988. Parishes throughout the 26-27 county diocese used these guidelines to write individual parish plans, taking into consideration the plans of neighboring parishes within a "cluster" grouping, so that a cluster plan would also be conceived. All of these plans were submitted to John in June 1989. The planning committee divided into seven two-person teams to evaluate the plans from the various regions of the diocese.

Earlier, in July 1987, John already had implemented an alternative staffing model by appointing two young priests as co-pastors of four parishes in northeast Kansas City. "Both the church and the northeast have experienced significant demographic and statistical shifts," he noted. "The numbers of parishioners in some parishes have declined significantly. The number of ordained priests available for ordained ministry has declined. We fully intend as a Catholic church to continue to serve the sacramental and other needs of the people in spite of these circumstances. In this diocese and throughout the world, the Catholic Church is developing creative and alternative ways of staffing our Catholic parishes and institutions. This is only a crisis if we name it a 'crisis.' If we call it an 'opportunity' it becomes an opportunity."

A sign of hope

In an address at the Bishop's Recognition Dinner for several hundred parishioners on Feb. 14, 1988, John added, "When I look at the signs of the times and planning, I am reminded of the quote of Cardinal (John) Dearden when he said, 'I not only do not have all the answers, I don't even know all the questions.' That's why it's so important that we have parishes doing self-studies and deaneries meeting together to develop a collaborative vision. These gatherings of parishes and deanery groups are a real sign of hope. . . . The parish self-study portion of planning is extremely tedious and difficult. Many pastors have told me that after some weeks the self-study was most revealing and gave them a much broader picture of their needs and the future. We must figure out a way to move into the 'preferred future,' rather than a future that simply happens to us . . . I encourage you to tell it like it is. In your reports and recommendations, I ask you to be specific and blunt. Please do not just recommend what you think the bishop or some committee wants to hear."

Seven subcommittees worked on writing the sections of the Framework for Parish Planning document: parish life and ministry; social outreach; Catholic schools; consultative bodies and the parish; parish finances/facilities/administration; ministerial personnel; and demographics. The guidelines noted that a parish pastoral council should be established and operative in every parish. Its purpose would be to unite laity, religious and clergy in a community of prayer, leadership, service and pastoral action. The guidelines also called for parishes to plan on having fewer priests and giving laypeople more ministerial responsibilities.

Watching and listening

In an introduction to the document, John wrote, "I will be watching and listening attentively as the parishes of the diocese try to come to grips with the problems which will be facing us over the next five or six years. I know that the difficulties we face are not easy to resolve. In some ways it may be easier to rest with the way things are today, rather than try to anticipate the future. However, it is my hope that parish planners would find creative and imaginative ways of using our resources of people and money, so that all of the Catholics in the diocese may be given the service they rightfully deserve."

The November 1988 planning guidelines estimated that the number of diocesan priests would diminish from 93 to 71 by 1991. Their ranks would be augmented by about 20 priests from religious orders. By 1991, the number of Catholics was projected to have fallen 30% (from 47,000 to 33,000) since 1970 in a district that included Kansas City's west side, central and northeast areas, and the city of St. Joseph. At the same time, the suburban Catholic population was to have grown by more than one-third, from 70,000 to 96,000.

On July 29, 1989, *The Kansas City Star* reported that 91 of 113 parishes in the diocese had drawn up plans to deal with the population shifts, a worsening priest shortage and the mounting costs of running a parish. The shortage of priests had already forced John to close three rural parishes at Braymer, Chula and Leopolis. The parish closings marked the fourth major change for the diocese since mid-1987 because of demographic shifts or financial problems. The other three were the assignment of the two-priest team in northeast Kansas City, the consolidation of the four central city schools and the appointment of Christian Brother Terrence McGlennon in June 1988 as the first non-ordained pastoral administrator in the diocese. He was assigned to Guardian Angels Parish in the Westport area of Kansas City.

The planning process resulted in 11 Kansas City parishes, primarily in the northeast and on the west side, merging into three in February 1991. The parish restructuring was officially announced Oct. 12, 1990, at a meeting of some 600 persons at St. John's Diocesan Center. One rural parish was closed, one mission parish was designated a chapel for weddings and funerals, and three rural parishes remained open as missions with no resident priest. A new parish north of the Missouri River in Kansas City was carved out and one rural parish was given permission to begin the process to build a new church. This meant that of the 27 counties in the diocese, 13 would have only one parish. John, in a letter to the people of the diocese, described the decision to close the parishes as "the most difficult decision since I've been your bishop."

Sister Jean Beste, chairperson of the diocesan planning committee, whom John in 1990 appointed director of the diocesan office of personnel and planning, says the main reason John decided on the closings and mergers was the shift in the Catholic population, especially in Kansas City. Central city parishes on the east side of the city lost 56% of their Catholic population between 1981 and 1989. The dwindling population left aging buildings and facilities under-utilized, while upkeep expenses rose. It also resulted in priests in the affected areas serving fewer people than was normal in other areas of the diocese.

Hard decisions

Throughout the planning process, John showed his trust in people, his willingness to make some hard decisions, and his humanness in experiencing painful changes, Sister Jean, a member of the Sisters of Charity of the Blessed Virgin Mary, assesses. "When we (diocesan planning committee) started, I don't really know if he knew the risk he was taking. He simply told us, 'I know we have to plan for the future, I don't know where to begin, but I know we have to do it.' And he would say over and over again, 'Involve people,' because that was important to him. . . . He trusted us and we all felt that very strongly."

She adds, "We spent several days going over the reports from the parish clusters. I couldn't believe he was willing to do this. It told me that in his mind these were very serious recommendations, and ultimately he knew he was going to take the heat because he was the bishop. So only he could make the final decisions. . . . He was willing to do it because he understood the future of the church in this diocese depended on it."

Sister Jean accompanied John to five regional meetings with diocesan priests in which the parish closings were discussed before a public announcement. "Bishop Sullivan said to the priests, 'I want to know if there's anybody who can't live with these decisions.' And then he waited to hear," she recalls. "There were some questions, but it was clear he had the support of most of his priests. I think this helped and it also really said something about him." When the closings were carried out, John "trusted his staff," Sister Jean adds. "I remember a couple of times he said, 'We can't close that parish because I don't know what to do with that priest and I have to work with personnel and you don't.' So it got a bit touchy. But he did have the broader picture and he knew the personality of his priests. So we had to respect him for his decisions, in light of all the things that he knew that we didn't. In all of it he was supportive, cooperative and trusting of his people. We could joke about it afterwards. He'd point to me and say 'She's the one who closed parishes.' "

Lasting impression

Sister Jean's lasting impression of John in relation to the entire planning process is that "he listened and he weighed things — probably too much — in the privacy of his own home, trying to figure out what to do. His personality was interesting because he would tell me a lot of things, but he wouldn't tell me his stance. It was difficult to read him sometimes. But that was his personality, that was his way, and once you knew that you could accept it. He wants people to like him. What people will think is very much a part of him."

Father Norman Rotert calls the parish restructuring painful, but "considerably less traumatic here than in other dioceses as a result of the planning process and the participation of people in the process." Father John Schuele, pastor of St. Therese, a central city parish, during the entire planning process, contends, "I've never heard or known of a bishop who said to his diocese, 'Look, here's the reality and how do you want to deal with it?' He wasn't in the process but he validated it. He gave the people that kind of process and that kind of power. He essentially ratified decisions . . . For us in the central city, it was especially difficult because we had seven parishes and we had a tortuous series of 24 meetings with representatives from all the parishes. I've never been through such a lengthy process. But we were working without precedent and without a model. And Bishop Sullivan's role in that was exemplary."

John's own sensitivity to the pain of people who lost places of gathering and worship, along with the skills and dedication of those assisting him, led to successful planning, contends Father William Bauman, pastor of Christ the King Parish in south Kansas City at the time. "It is impressive to me that we could close and consolidate nearly 14% of our parish communities and never make the national press. Movements of people made the closings and consolidations necessary; Bishop Sullivan felt the pain as much as anyone in the diocese; the future, the vision demanded that decisions be made — and they were made."

Just and living wages

A significant piece of the planning process was a four-year plan, announced Jan. 12, 1988 by John to priests, principals and diocesan leaders, to guarantee "just and living" wages for persons working in pastoral and educational ministries in the diocese. The proposal was recommended to John by a task force appointed by the priests' finance committee in the fall of 1987 to examine salaries for all diocesan employees. The plan demanded that professional, full-time personnel in diocesan agencies, parishes and schools be assigned a salary range which takes into account the position held, the education and experience of the employee, and the competition of the marketplace.

The plan, to be carried out from 1989 to 1992, set as a goal that by 1991 salaries for teachers in diocesan schools would achieve a level in excess of 80% of local public school salaries. It set also as a goal that by 1991 all full-time lay ministers with master's degrees who had several years' experience and significant leadership responsibility would receive salaries ranging from $25,000 to $30,000 annually. At the time, there were some 1,200 ministers in the diocese. Of this number, 10% were priests, 30% were religious sisters and brothers, and 60% were full-time lay personnel, including more than 650 lay teachers in schools and about 50 lay professionals working in parishes.

The cost of implementing the salaries plan was projected at $3.6 million over four years. The money would be raised primarily through an increase in offertory collections in parishes. John asked the task force to include specifically the goal that a religious sister or brother working in the diocese would receive the same salary as a lay employee with equal qualifications, responsibility and experience. John said also it was his intent to establish a personnel office for the diocese which would be responsible for all personnel files, evaluations and contracts with diocesan employees. "Without a consensus among all of us about this plan, change will not be possible," John emphasized to leaders at the January 1988 meeting. "The only 'if' in this plan is a consensus among the clergy, and really doing what we all feel is practical and should be done.

"In my 43 years as a parish priest and bishop, this is the most serious and crucial decision I have ever had to face. And because of the grave pastoral implications, you (pastors, principals and diocesan leaders) must share this decision and its consequences with me. . . . We cannot speak about the American bishops' pastoral on the U.S. economy with sincerity and persuasion unless we live justly. However, I do not advocate spending money that we do not have on hand. I do not like to operate at a deficit — it's just not sound. We must undertake only what we can afford. And we must make an all-out effort to determine what we can afford and raise. I have great faith in the efficacy of prayer and in your commitment, but I think our potential here is going to be greatly tested."

Father Bauman, chairman of the task force on salaries, recalls that John "endorsed the salaries concept with some courage, but it took a little doing. It was sort of a threat against restoring financial security. I think the plan at first really scared him. In order to keep quality schools and for them to survive, that meant a 40% increase in salaries over a three-year period. So as we laid it out, he struggled with it. In later years he would look back on this and take great pride, but I always had the feeling in the beginning that I wasn't making his day."

The diocesan school system "is bigger and much better since we instituted the plan," Father Bauman concludes. "We are maintaining our employees. People who work in the schools and parishes say it's worth working here because the diocese is paying a just wage. It was a brave step to say we would pay a just wage and define what the criteria were, but Bishop Sullivan saw it through."

Appoints pastoral administrator

Concurrent with the planning process, John announced also in January 1988 that he would appoint the first non-ordained pastoral administrator of a parish in June 1988, in conjunction with other clergy changes. "We need some time to assess this new development in ministry," he said. "We need to live with it awhile to understand the problems. Thus, even while we have enough priests to serve the parishes, I wish to do this." He noted that the potential number of priests who could retire in the near future remained very high in proportion to the total number of diocesan priests. Those being ordained would not replace those who were sick or would retire. "A positive feature of the lay administrator is that priests will have the freedom to take sabbaticals, and to enter other types of ministry that they could not if they had to be in parishes full-time," he said.

At the installation of Brother Terrence McGlennon as pastoral administrator of Guardian Angels Church in Kansas City on June 21, 1988, John said that like Abraham, Brother Terry was called to go into a strange land — he didn't know where he was going or exactly what his role was, but his faith motivated him to respond. John, who had appointed

Brother Terry to this new position after he had served as diocesan youth ministry director for several years, told him not to reduce his ambition to be an excellent administrator, but "above all, be a man of faith, the efficacious sign that God cares."

John appointed also a committee of priests and diocesan ministry leaders to research the ministry of pastoral administrator and to make recommendations for implementing it in the diocese. The committee was chaired by George Noonan, director of the Center for Pastoral Life and Ministry. Among its members were Jesuit Father Kevin Cullen, who served with Brother Terry as associate pastor of Guardian Angels Parish, and Sister Ellen Morseth, BVM, of the Center's staff, who had been a pastoral administrator for seven years prior to coming to the Kansas City-St. Joseph diocese.

Diocesan standards and qualifications for the role of pastoral administrator were approved by John and the presbyterial council on Dec. 14, 1990, after a two-year study by the committee. The committee saw the role "as a particular response to the call to discipleship." Their report said the pastoral administrator "is entrusted with the pastoral care of a local parish community. This does not necessarily imply that the pastoral administrator is the person that actually performs all of the tasks involved in the life of the parish, but rather that many will be exercised through collaboration and delegation." The report emphasized that the pastoral administrator was appointed by the bishop to pastoral and administrative responsibilities for a parish, as encouraged by Vatican II and made possible by the Code of Canon Law (517.2).

Tensions confronted

The appointment of a pastoral administrator carried with it some tensions. Some diocesan leaders thought John, who promoted the concept among other bishops, was slow in implementing it in his own diocese. "Naturally there were people who opposed the concept, but that had nothing to do with who was going to be appointed or who the bishop was. They were going to oppose it no matter what," Noonan says. "It always amazed me that the man (John) who was such an advocate of lay ministry couldn't make a faster move. I got frustrated because we had the systems set up and had made recommendations as to how the pastoral administrator should be introduced into the parish. But I saw his reluctance as the 'old part' of John Sullivan. He was still a little hesitant about moving forward on some things.

"It's disappointing that we don't have more pastoral administrators appointed (there are two in the diocese now) because we have some good and talented priests who just don't want to be pastors," Noonan adds. "Some of them are excellent presiders and preachers but don't feel that they have the gifts to pastor a parish. At the same time, I believe that within the ranks of our lay pastoral ministers, we do have some who would be very capable of taking on the role of pastoral leadership in a parish. I think that Bishop Sullivan was just nervous. If you study the whole history of the appointment of (Brother) Terry, it was a mess. Not because we didn't know what we were doing, but because there was that tension — we kept asking if we were really going to do this. One of the facts of life is that there are many parts that make up who we are. I guess that Bishop Sullivan ultimately opted for what he felt was right, but that didn't mean that he liked every facet of it. He didn't go into this blindly. He was much more balanced than many of the priests thought he was in arriving at his decision."

Father Richard Carney, diocesan chancellor, assesses that John was "very much for the idea (of pastoral administrators) and saw it coming, but I think he was not wanting to offend — again it was his gentleness. He was secure about the reaction of the laity, but he was quite certain it was going to cause a stir among the priests. So while in theory he was very much for it, he never was secure enough to say, 'OK, this is it.' And he would consider no one but Brother Terry because he already had his own personal impression of him . . . That was both a blessing and a curse for him." Christian Brother Michael Fehrenbach, a close friend of Brother Terry (who died in 1991), assesses that John was "afraid at times to go ahead, even though he had a great deal of trust in Terry. The pastoral administrator concept promoted a vision of church that Bishop Sullivan had been talking about, but the priesthood was also so important to him. . . . He was caught up in the reaction of the people. Sometimes he would be paralyzed by it and act against his own best instincts."

Divided over concept

The priests' personnel board was divided over the pastoral administrator concept, and this had an impact on John's thinking, says Father John Schuele. "We had priests who said, 'By God, as long as we have priests, let's assign a priest.' For about two years, Bishop Sullivan said, 'Wait a minute, you guys, the future shows we're going to have to appoint a pastoral administrator because we just don't have the priests.' But when it came to crunch time, he very definitely had hesitations about it. He never articulated those, so I'm not sure what was going through his mind. I don't know what kinds of pressures he was under. We don't know what the other bishops told him. There were other rural dioceses that had years of experience. They may have said, 'Jack, it doesn't work very well.' We just don't know. . . . While he would endorse the concept, it took him a long time to put it into practice."

"In my mind," John says today, "I knew we were a sacramental church, that we've got to have the Eucharist, but that there was tremendous change coming and we had to prepare for it. We were not as bad off as some of the other dioceses as far as the number of priests and resources. One thing I have learned is that the qualities of the sacramental minister working with the pastoral administrator have to be extraordinary. It takes a very special man with noble character. It takes a person who's willing to sit in the second row."

Women in ministry

During John's last decade as bishop of Kansas City-St. Joseph, women's involvement in the church increased at a rapid rate. Laywomen and women religious were changing the church in the diocese and across the country, sometimes with great support and sometimes against considerable obstacles. John appointed women to key diocesan roles, including superintendent of schools, editor of *The Catholic Key* (diocesan newspaper), director of the personnel and planning office, and defender of the bond on the marriage tribunal. Despite these advances, he told *Kansas City Magazine* in a May 1986 interview, "Women make changes in the liturgy at some churches and, immediately, a letter goes to Rome. Then Rome writes a letter. As bishop, I'm caught in the middle in a sort of Catch-22."

John was well-known for "his emphasis on women in ministry, his openness to women in ministry, and his willingness to place women in important positions in the chancery and in parishes," says Father Norman Rotert. "He strongly encouraged women playing a major role in parish staffing. He brought this with him from Grand Island. Before he got here, I had already heard about this John Sullivan who was attracting nuns from all over the country to work in Grand Island. The word was out there, and it was out here that if you go to John Sullivan's diocese as a woman, you're going to be able to function."

John's collaborative relationship with women religious extended back to his days as a pastor in Oklahoma. Over his years as a bishop, he continued to examine the relationship. "The full meaning of the bishop in his relationship to women religious has not yet emerged," he noted in a homily for the Leadership Conference of Women Religious in August 1984. "I do not know with certainty what the future holds for either of us in terms of our mutual responsibilities, undertakings, supports and obligations. For all of us in church leadership the coming years will be challenging — years in which new meanings are forged, years in which new structures will evolve . . . Whatever else I know about the future, I do know this. We will be called to give more than we think we can give. When we think we have nothing left, we will still be called to give whatever we have. We will be called to take risks."

During the mid-1980s, women religious and laywomen in the diocese formed a group for dialogue and education called the Conference of Church Women. The group sponsored forums on women's concerns in 1986 and 1987, and reviewed the U.S. bishops' drafts for a pastoral letter on women's concerns. They also met with John on an ongoing basis to talk about women's needs and concerns in the diocese.

In a short address to some 100 participants in one of the forums on women's concerns in November 1986, John noted that although the teaching of the church opposing the ordination of women to the priesthood was clear, the Catholic community must "pursue every other avenue to remedy the present inequality that exists in the church." To pursue ordination as the only alternative to church inequality "would only frustrate and be counterproductive."

Ecclesial bonding

"It is my belief that the issues of women which are in the limelight today are very real and they deserve to be in the limelight," John said. "I am in complete sympathy with the efforts of those who choose to dialogue and discuss these issues in an effort to reach deeper understanding; understanding is the necessary prelude to a deeper integration of women into the structures of the church." The growth of the church will depend largely on "ecclesial bonding" that can come about by a genuine collaboration among diocesan clergy, women and men religious, and the laity, he added. "We need to work toward a balanced understanding of a Catholic church that recognizes the rightful place of the clergy, religious and laity, and men and women equally. By maintaining the balance in who participates in church we are able then to develop and maintain a balanced ecclesiology. To eliminate or ignore any one of these elements of church would be a gross error."

On his 10th anniversary as bishop of Kansas City-St. Joseph in August 1987, John reflected on his role in the contemporary church in an interview with *The Catholic Key.* "People really expect you to be so many things — administrator, enabler, teacher and shepherd — and there's no way in which you can be all those things," he said. "But I think one of the most important characteristics of a bishop today is his vision of church, and second, he must possess a tremendous trust in the goodness and providence of God . . . The trust I cite here is not only in God's goodness, but trust in people. A bishop has to be very personal . . . (being) a bishop is sometimes a lonely existence. I find that one of the most important sources of support which keeps me going as a person is the affection of the priests, religious and laypeople. Maybe that sounds funny, but I'm human and you can't function without friends and the support of others."

A continual struggle for John throughout his tenure in Kansas City-St. Joseph was a perceived lack of support and acceptance by some of the diocesan priests, partly as a result of their reaction to his emphasis on lay ministry and his ideas about the changing role of the priesthood. As early as June 1984, in his address to priests at the closing of the diocesan Emmaus program, John acknowledged the gulf and his shortcomings. "Ideally, I would like to be as understanding, as articulate, as intelligent, as creative, as blessed, as sympathetic a leader as you deserve. Believe me, the gulf between the ideal bishop you warrant, and the real John Sullivan which you have is incredibly more painful for me to endure than it is for you. I am sorry the breadth of the gulf between the ideal and the real is, in this case, so wide. I ask for your understanding. At times, I beg for your forgiveness."

Priests are a priority

In the August 1987 interview, John noted, "Priests are always a priority in a bishop's life, but I am especially concerned about the perception that priests have of their future role. While some see it as being exclusively liturgical, actually the priest in the future will be called upon to provide direction and leadership to possibly a cluster of parishes, and his role will be similar to that of a bishop. The priest's qualities should be those that we listed for a bishop: vision, trust, discipline, and being a man of prayer."

That not all of the diocesan priests supported John's efforts in lay ministry was a source of great suffering to him, contends Father Norman Rotert. "So many priests felt that he (John) had been neglectful of the priests during his episcopacy," he says. "But I think basically it flows from their insecurity. There was a need to emphasize the role of the laity and the bishop certainly acknowledged that. And in emphasizing the role of the laity, he did pay a heavy price with a lot of the priests.

"When John came to the diocese, he strongly emphasized the role of women and women religious, particularly in the parishes," Father Rotert adds. "He wanted multiple ministries in parishes and wanted parishes to develop competent staffs, and he pushed this very hard. There were a lot of priests who didn't understand how to do that. And they saw it as threatening of their role. So they felt Bishop Sullivan was uncaring about them. Some of them have changed their opinion over time, but there's still a substantial number of priests that feel this way."

The reaction of diocesan priests to expanding ministry opportunities for women religious and laity was sometimes defensiveness, John says, because "over the years we conditioned priests to want their own turf. I was trying to say we're in a church that's in a state of change, and there was an intolerance to this, even among the clergy. Some were ready to do battle. Women religious in many cases were so far ahead because they had had the continuing education opportunities and the priests did not. So many of the priests resisted to save face and they're still resisting."

A traditional priest

George Noonan says that because John was in many ways a traditional priest — "a product of his own culture and formation" — "it always wounded him when priests felt he was not supportive of them. I don't think they realized how supportive of them he really was, frequently at a cost to the laity.

"He absolutely placed the interests of priests first," Noonan adds. "They don't believe it. While he had tremendous openness to laity, his instincts still leaned toward priests. I think that in his own career he would have felt happier if more priests had patted him on the back for the direction he went. He never pulled away from his vision, but I think it always wounded him. He sought the acceptance of priests because that's the milieu that he was formed in — their acceptance is what mattered to him."

John's "engendering of the empowerment of the laity wasn't in a vacuum and distinct from his respect for the value of the ordained priesthood," Noonan concludes. "I don't think you're going to find many bishops as supportive of lay ministry as he is, but he is still a product of his time. He believed that you needed a broad ministering community, so that you don't burn out any particular category — especially the ordained ministry."

John's relationship with priests was a "mixed issue," contends Father William Bauman. "Right up until the end, there was a sense among some of the priests that they had been somewhat betrayed, because of the voice that was given to lay ministers and to women religious. There was a strong group of priests, about 50%, who were saying that this was the right way to go. So I think that was a split in the clergy, and probably we grew through the split . . . From start to finish, Bishop Sullivan was such a feeling person. He approached everything with that passion and feeling — that was a beautiful thing. It also meant that he suffered many things more than other people would."

Father John Schuele viewed the distance between John and some of the priests as "a sad thing that didn't have to happen. For myself, personally, I didn't see the emphasis on lay ministry as mutually exclusive. He was very supportive of his priests, so I could never see how people could reach that conclusion. But there were some priests who were alienated."

Father Richard Carney, who served as both a pastor and diocesan chancellor during John's tenure, says "the priests never faulted Bishop Sullivan as a person for trying. They were just unclear on the concept of multiple ministries and somewhat threatened. . . . As laypeople were becoming more involved, some priests felt less valued. That was threatening to a lot of priests. No one wanted to be a circuit rider just running from parish to parish saying Mass every Sunday.

"Bishop Sullivan didn't feel that anything extraordinary was going to become of the priests' lives," Father Carney adds. "He knew they were going to have to be more adept at personnel management. Many only had a housekeeper and a janitor, and now they were going to have to learn different skills . . . Partially it was a gut reaction — and that's why it was emotional. But it did address questions that we are still struggling with about the role of the priest. Bishop Sullivan addressed it early on — it created a lot of anxiety, without an eventual answer to all the questions."

Listening sessions

Father Michael Roach, who was ordained in 1981 and later served on the diocesan priestly life and ministry committee, recalls attending listening sessions where "some priests were really hurting. But I think they were taking their own personal anger, confusion and tension out on Bishop Sullivan. They said they didn't support him. I think that was just the role of the priest at the time. They were dealing with a lot of personal issues, yet blaming Bishop Sullivan for not having a vision of the priesthood."

In contrast to those who felt a lack of support, there were some diocesan priests who felt secure with John's ideas and valued the trust he placed in his pastors. "We just hit it off from the beginning," says Father Schuele. "I thought he was an interesting character. I came to discover that the person he was in public was the person he really was. I discovered that the warmth he conveyed was genuine. I always considered him a personal friend. I never felt any hesitation to go to him with anything, and he was always extraordinarily open with me.

"He would intuitively seize what he thought were good ideas," Father Schuele notes. "And people can read that about him, especially in his earlier days . . . So he affected a lot of people with that kind of style. And again it was genuine. He set a tone by that. . . . Pastorally, I think he mastered the fine art of looking the other way. I can't think of a higher compliment for a bishop. For me personally, that's one thing I want from a bishop — I don't want a bishop 'nickel-and-diming' me. Never in all those years — and we were involved in some experimental things, perhaps some questionable things — have I known him to discipline anyone unless it were the most flagrant kind of violation. He really entrusted our parishes to us as pastors, and that's a great feeling."

Father Bauman, who eventually succeeded two "untouchable" pastors who refused to be moved by John during the clergy changes in 1978, recalls, "I felt total confidence that my bishop supported me in the way I approached parish ministry. That was particularly important when I was sent to Christ the King Parish were Msgr. Kearney had been, because that had been a problem that was very painful to him.

There were some very hateful beginnings that took a long time to turn around. I always remember Bishop Sullivan being very supportive when people would write to him about me. He would call me in to look at the letters . . . At one point he even offered me a move, knowing that I was in some pain — to say that if I was burning out, he didn't want to leave me there to die. He had the sensitivity to let me make the decision."

Father Gerald Waris, who was ordained a priest 10 years when John came to Kansas City-St. Joseph, recalls how John's relationship with the priests changed over his years as bishop. "Probably because of my own insecurity, I was apprehensive at first about what his relationship with the priests would be. It took a while, but once we became more comfortable with him we became less anxious about our own welfare. But I think there were some anxious times — some of it was misunderstanding, and whether there were feelings that we were not cared for or nurtured, I'm not really sure."

Harshly criticized

"In some ways, I feel like Bishop Sullivan was harshly criticized," Father Waris adds. "He gave you an assignment to do the best you could. He allowed you the freedom to accomplish those things you felt this parish was calling you to, that Christ was calling you to. I felt like I had the freedom to implement his vision. This was to his credit — he gave you the freedom to use your creative powers, your God-given talents, to move a parish beyond the comfortable."

Two marks of John's interaction with diocesan clergy over the years were his personal placement of priests by intuition as opposed to broad consultation, and his struggle in confronting his priests in conflicting situations. Father Rotert contends that John had a unique skill, particularly in his early years as bishop, of sensing the appropriate people for the appropriate jobs, and this extended to his selection of pastors. "In working with him, he would have hunches about something — he couldn't explain why he felt this way about a person, but in hindsight almost always his hunches were correct. So his intuitions were just outstanding," he says.

Father Bauman remembers that at the time of the controversial clergy changes in 1978, the diocesan clergy recognized John's right to make those changes without the formal process of a priests' personnel board. "Then gradually, over the next 15 years, the priests fought back to get a personnel board they wanted," Father Bauman says. "I think many of us felt that in his first 10 years, when he had more priest personnel to work with, he was extremely successful in putting people in the right places. . . . It was very hard on him in the last few years when he had such a shortage of priests. He found himself filling slots, and not happy that he matched the right man with the right job, but he had moved everyone so often that he just couldn't move them anymore. It was part of the cost of a diminishing priesthood."

John had a good instinct about placing priests in a parish, says Father Patrick Rush. "The problem was that left us without any kind of policy regarding priest personnel, and that's not an empowering kind of situation — it's rather a de-powering or disability situation . . . Many times in our gatherings he would say he'd want parishes with strong liturgies or adult education programs, but almost never in our assignments did he say, 'Now this is why I think you'd be good at that parish and this is what I'd like to see happen.' I think that emotions on the part of some people reacted to this."

Pastors set a tone

Father Schuele, who served several years on the priests' personnel board, contends that John had a passion about the assignment of priests to parishes. "He really felt that parishes were where the church is, and pastors set a tone for a parish. There were many very painful times on the personnel board, trying to match up parishes with priests. I know it was a tremendous personal burden for him, because he hated to press a priest to go somewhere. When a priest told him no, he hurt, and he would anguish about it. He really did try to respect the priests' wishes; he bent over backwards. But that's not going to show up in the public forum."

While placement of priests brought John pain, it also brought him joy, Father Schuele adds. "I would tease him — you know some guys play horses, some play cards, you play personnel. When an assignment seemed to be working, he would mention it with pride. . . . I know the priests as a group said some pretty disparaging things. And something I heard continually was they thought Sullivan wasn't open to the personnel board's ideas. That was the furthest from the truth. He would beg us for ideas . . . He wasn't always free to say everything, because as bishop he knew confidential things — that was the nature of it and he didn't violate it. But he would press us to be forthcoming with our ideas."

Father Waris calls John's intuition about priests "his greatest virtue and his biggest weakness. I think he wanted to do his very best to get every priest in the right place. It was hard for him to let go of control of that. His difficulty was making it a process whereby assignments could be made with a little more involvement of parishes and staff. I could criticize this but I also could live with it." Adds Father Michael Roach, "Some priests were irked by his (John's) style, but I always felt very affirmed. He knew me and my gifts and strengths and where they would be the best served. I trusted that, but I know that some didn't feel there was much consultation — which there wasn't. But I realized that wasn't a strength of his."

Expresses his dilemma

John expressed his own dilemma of priests' placements during a gathering of diocesan clergy at Conception Abbey in October 1988. "Some weeks ago I was forcefully reminded of how much I care for you (priests) personally when I was so devastated by those listening sessions in which four deaneries had adverse comments 'about the relationship our priests have with the bishop,'" John said. "It took me a long time to recover and reflect on this question . . . We — the personnel board and I — would be dealing with a much easier task if it were a case of dealing with only priests who are willing to move. The task is much more difficult than that. Even priests willing to move are not willing to move just *anyplace*; that's understandable. But often a priest willing to move is willing to move to parish A but not B, though B is open and A is not.

"Admittedly, there is a bias in favor of the right man for the parish rather than the right parish for the man . . . As bishop I have to try to strike a balance between what the priest feels and what I judge the parish *needs* as pastor. That's a bias a bishop *must* have. Sometimes it happens that a priest has a view of his competency in a particular kind of ministry that he may well have but has not ever indicated that to me or the personnel board. That information also changes. Priests have said to me that they want, for instance, a rural parish, and were incensed when they were assigned to one. They changed their minds . . . but we didn't know it! . . . Clergy changes are *seldom* initiated by me; they are usually precipitated by ordinations, or retirement, or death or illness. It is not a case then that I *like* to make moves just for moves' sakes; I make moves because the situations of priests demand moves. Being realistic about clergy appointments is a duty of the bishop, but being realistic about one's move is incumbent on the priest too!"

John's personality was a hindrance in his ability to confront priests when he thought there might be resistance, according to Father Carney. "If Bishop Sullivan felt that a priest should do something but he anticipated his resistance, he would always back off from saying anything," he says. "That was a problem sometimes, but it goes back to his sincere gentleness as a person. His person and psyche need to avoid any conflict . . . He would create buffers between himself and any negativity. Sometimes this inhibited him from doing the things that did involve courage and forthrightness. It is a piece of his character and personality that inhibits problems from being addressed. It is not a criticism of him personally, but it is an example of how someone's personality enters into the role of being a bishop." John "certainly was reluctant to confront some of the priests about what he disliked," adds Father Schuele. "I can remember him saying about one priest, 'Oh God, he's told me no six times.' And I said, 'I think you're taking it personally.'"

"Sullivan as a human being was beloved as a human being," Father Patrick Rush contends. "Maybe there were a few people who had grudges that couldn't even see that, but as a man whose weaknesses were obvious to us as well as his strengths, I think he was a much beloved person. I think an appeal like that is an appeal to one's humanity."

The good shepherd

Father Rush adds, "I know instances where he worked with priests or people who were in very compromised situations. I have icons from that time of what the good shepherd is like. He epitomized in those times — once he got over his anger, it betrays the Irish in him and he takes it personally — what Christianity is all about. He told me, 'Well, you know, it could have been me in that situation.' And I think he really believed that. That is the wonderfully warm, human, compassionate side of John Sullivan."

John showed such a side at the clergy days at Conception Abbey in October 1988 when he told the priests, "I want all of you to know that I am always available and want you to feel free to speak with me anytime and on any subject. One time I heard a chancery observer in Chicago say the difference between Cardinal Stritch and his successor, Cardinal Meyer, was that Stritch was a layman's bishop and Meyer a priests' bishop. I idolized Albert Gregory Meyer and wish, probably futilely, that I could be remembered as a priests' bishop. . . . This 'priests' bishop' was the greatest single support I had in the (Extension) lay volunteer program. He was a good theologian and pastor and had unusual insights into the coming role and ministry of the laity. In spite of rather constant criticism I receive about talking too much about lay ministry and how this is a threat to many ordained ministers, I am proud of what is happening in our diocese."

John added, "I experience all the same frustrations, uncertainties, loneliness and even anger that you know and possibly even more. Some priests distrust me in a big way, even some religious women seriously misinterpret what I try to do; laity and others complain by letter and in person to the (papal) nuncio about my so-called leadership style and how I don't (they say) enforce the law. I am supposed to be and hope to be a pastor and not simply a law enforcer. All this stuff and much more hurts."

In the last few years before his retirement, John took personally and with great struggle some of the current problems facing diocesan priests, including the resignation of priests who wished to marry, priests dying from AIDS, and charges of clergy sexual abuse. On the latter issue, he insisted on the development of diocesan procedures and policies on responding to claims of sexual abuse that were put in effect in May 1988.

A pastor at heart

"When priests left the ministry or died of AIDS, Bishop Sullivan took it very personally, even though it was not his fault," says Father Carney. "He didn't always talk about it a lot. These things really hurt him more in terms of, 'What should I have done more, what if I had known more,' and him feeling an awful lot of guilt about it and a terrible personal hurt. He had magnanimous understanding, patience and compassion for priests who were in trouble. In fact, we used to tease him — if you really want to get the bishop's attention, you've got to get in trouble. He was gentle, fatherly, forgiving — all the best in the man came out for some kind of renegade. He was a pastor at heart."

John "took any priests' issues very personally and to heart," adds Father Michael Roach. "I know that two priests dying of AIDS was a factor, and we had a number leave who were young priests, and he took that personally. I think that's just where the church is, but often times that's too threatening."

In one case of sexual abuse allegations against a young priest in early 1993, John wrote to parishioners of a suburban parish "with a heavy heart." He said, "It is shocking to hear such allegations made against an acquaintance. It is traumatizing when it is a priest to whom you have given your love and your trust. I want you to know that I hurt and I cry with you. I am deeply concerned about the children and the families whose lives are in turmoil over this matter. . . . The fullness of healing requires time and God's work in all of us: the victims, the accused, the hurting families, the parish community and the people of the diocese."

Early retirement

Since the late 1980s, John had suffered from Parkinson's disease, a progressive neurological disorder that made it difficult for him to walk and move. He had told the diocesan priests about his disease in the fall of 1992. It was John's poor health and diminishing energy that caused him at age 72 to submit his resignation before the customary age of 75. He wrote to Pope John Paul II on June 30, 1992. He revealed the news of his resignation in a letter delivered to priests and diocesan employees dated January 12, 1993, while he and close friend Father Bill Swift were on vacation in Florida.

In a letter to the people of the diocese read at Masses on Jan. 16-17, John wrote, "Given the greater challenges and opportunities for service that characterize our situation, and my diminishing level of energy due to my illness, I thought it best for the welfare of the church and the broader community in our 27-county diocese that I relinquish my office at this time." He said he was particularly grateful "to all those who have picked up the mantle of mature responsibility as Christians — the priests and religious and the lay women and men who have responded to the challenges our times present."

John told *The Kansas City Star* in an interview that he appreciated all people in the diocese, both Catholic and non-Catholic. "That's something I cherish very much, the openness, or the response, I've received from the whole population," he said. "That's a great treasure. I've tried in my own human — rather weak — way to lead, but not to push. To invite, but not to demand." In addition, he told *The Catholic Key* that serving in a diocese with both urban and rural areas allowed him "to know people. You see people more than once, so you can establish relationships . . . I have experienced the greatest sensitivity among the people to the needs of one another and to the needs of all. It's a measure of the health of the faith community. It's extraordinary."

John added that he was "personally grateful for the willingness to makes changes" to bring about the post-conciliar church. "Some may have been reluctant," he said, and Vatican II did raise great expectations, "but it's not over." Another indication of the faith of the people, he said, is "the way they support us financially. We have eliminated a large debt, added a pension fund and we have not curtailed services, even though some of our most financially well-off people have moved to Kansas suburbs over the years."

Asked to identify some accomplishments which he found particularly pleasing, John noted, "I am delighted with the growth and progress that we have made in training and formation for all ministry through the Center for Pastoral Life and Ministry. We don't do this because of the declining numbers of priests and religious, but for doctrinal reasons. By virtue of our baptism and confirmation all of us — ordained and non-ordained — have a responsible role in the church.

That role can be summarized as making the love of God tangible to all people."

Challenges are formidable

With regard to the future of the church, John said, "I'm optimistic, and that's not just a company line. As I've said many times before, we are not involved in just a human enterprise. We are dealing with the mystery of God's church. The challenges are formidable. The problem is tremendous. And the solution will have to be proportional to the problem. The answer lies in God's grace, and will have something to do with people's generosity in responding to our mission of making God's love audible, visible and tangible."

John told the *St. Joseph News-Press* in March 1993 that his plans for retirement were to "do what I've been doing all along, but with a clear conscience, because you're always worrying about people." He said he'd miss "people getting on your case, probably. It's a crisis existence. You always think, 'If I can just live until Tuesday, everything's going to be all right.' And Tuesday comes, and you have a whole new package of questions. What will I miss the most? I think dealing with the people and the priests of the diocese. I have an awful time being alone. Put it this way: I enjoy very much being out with the people. And I will miss that."

John's close friend, Archbishop John May of St. Louis, had also been forced to retire early at age 71 in December 1992 because of brain cancer. Some of John's fellow bishops felt that John dealt with his own illness and early retirement with "predictable grace." John's "sense of humor not only benefitted others, it benefitted him during this challenging time," says Bishop John Leibrecht, bishop of Springfield-Cape Girardeau, Missouri. "John had some real disappointments in life and also physical pain. Somehow his sense of humor would show up in the midst of that and give him perspective. It was more helpful to him than he probably realizes. It helped him face his resignation. I'm convinced it was his sense of humor that gave him the perspective that his retiring was best for the church. That's how he thinks — what's best for the church is always his priority and this helped him personally as well as in his relationship with others."

Cardinal Bernard Law of Boston, Massachusetts contends that John "has borne the burden of illness with predictable grace and it's saddened all of us who know and love him. That John should experience this kind of physical disability has certainly shown all of us how to deal with illness. His own preparation for retirement and easing the transition to his successor — all this is a mark of the great sense of church that he has and has always had."

Successor appointed

John announced the appointment of his successor, Bishop Raymond J. Boland of Birmingham, Alabama, on June 22, 1993 in a press conference at the diocesan chancery. In a prepared statement, he said he was "content and pleased" at the appointment of Bishop Boland. "I am grateful to the Holy Father, Pope John Paul II, for his gracious acceptance of my letter of resignation and his paternal understanding of my need to step down from the responsibilities as bishop," he added. Pledging to assist the new bishop in any way needed, he said, "I can step aside with relief and much peace of mind and heart . . . I feel hopeful in the Lord for the future of our beloved, local church."

Several hundred people from throughout the diocese gathered in the Cathedral of the Immaculate Conception on August 8, 1993 to say thank you and farewell to John for the last time as their bishop. Many speakers praised John for his keen wit, great energy and an always-present sense of humor. They said he loved jokes — "good and bad" — and was always ready to tell a story, even if it got in the way of a meeting agenda. "Thank you for being our bishop," said Jim Tierney, longtime diocesan attorney. "And thank you for being our friend."

Human compassion

But mainly, John was honored for his human compassion and an unyielding social conscience. He was called a powerful voice for the oppressed and the poor and lauded for his commitment to the inner city schools. "He preached that the poor shall enjoy a priority — especially the children," said Father Norman Rotert in a talk during the celebration. For those convictions, John was sometimes made to suffer, Father Rotert added. For example, John's insistence that the church send increased funding to poverty-stricken areas "was not popular everywhere." But John "said everyone must be a minister, because you may be the only gospel someone ever hears."

The Scripture passage chosen for the retirement celebration was one of John's favorites, taken from the letter from Paul to the Philippians (1:3-11): "I thank God every time I remember you, constantly praying with joy in every one of my prayers for all of you, because of your sharing in the Gospel from the first day until now. I am confident of this, that the one who began the good work among you will bring it to completion by the day of Jesus Christ . . . And this is my prayer, that your love may overflow more and more with knowledge and full insight to help you determine what is best, so that in the day of Christ you may be pure and blameless, having produced the harvest of righteousness that comes through Jesus Christ for the glory and praise of God."

Father Rotert, comparing John to the apostle Paul who was writing from prison, noted John "has had Parkinson's disease for the last several years and has served us from that confinement. I suppose that at times the episcopacy has felt like a kind of confinement. . . . Bishop Sullivan calls all of us to share in the mission of the church. He takes great joy in the response of the people of this diocese, who not only serve with enthusiasm, but serve competently. . . . Bishop Sullivan loved us. He has called us to a life of love and understanding and to know what to do."

In a farewell address, John issued a plea on behalf of children: "The future is in the hands of those who can give our youth reasons for living . . . Your role as baptized Christians is to make God's infinite love tangible and visible here and now . . . There are only two things in this world that last, two things worth cultivating: people and the relationship that exists between people. Heaven is union with Our Lord and with one another, and it is forever."

Since John's retirement on Sept. 9, 1993, when Bishop Boland was installed as the fifth bishop of Kansas City-St. Joseph, there have been many assessments of his 16 years of service to the diocese.

He is greatly different

What distinguishes bishops "are the personal and personality traits that translate into their style of governance," contends Father Carney. "In that, Bishop Sullivan is no different and, in another way, he is greatly different. He is a man deeply loving of people, all kinds of people. That is why he remembers them, calls them by name long after having first been introduced, knows poignant little personal things about them, is cordial and at ease with people, and they with him. This is not a politician's campaign with him; it is deep interest and genuine concern that he demonstrates.

"Years ago he was convinced of the value for the church that is the laity," Father Carney adds. "That, undoubtedly, marks the reason for his strong conviction of the value of lay leadership and ministry. If there is one single effort that he has initiated and sustained with enthusiasm, it is his commitment to lay ministry. Our local church has profited much from that guidance and the resultant efforts of thousands whose lives and skills have touched other's lives.

"You learn the personal traits of a bishop after awhile and you become a translator. 'No' was a word Bishop Sullivan hated to use; it was just too harsh a word for his kindly manner. Many, if not most of the laity of the diocese got to know Bishop Sullivan in a personal, comfortable way that few had previously known any bishop."

John's been "a bishop with a vision that is very appropriate to the time in which we live," concludes Father Rotert, perhaps John's closest friend while bishop. "In a high-tech society and in a society that is experiencing considerable alienation of people, it's very appropriate for a spiritual leader to be a warm, compassionate, loving leader."

CHAPTER EIGHT

A Vision of Lay Ministry — The Center for Pastoral Life and Ministry and the Institute for Pastoral Life

LONG BEFORE THERE WAS A RECOGNIZED PRIEST SHORTAGE IN the United States, John was convinced of the importance of lay leaders working side by side with priests and religious in parishes. Shaped deeply by his experiences as a pastor in Oklahoma, by the witness of the Extension Volunteers, by the spirit of Vatican II and by the team ministry in Grand Island, by the late 1970s he had a vision of what parishes could become — places of loving ministry and care.

His vision of lay ministry that developed over three decades, John says, was grounded in the value of people as individuals and a belief in their inherent dignity, importance and sacredness. "When one accepts people, not as *numbers* but as *mysteries*, then one's attitude toward ministry, one's attitude toward the church, one's ecclesiology, one's spirituality, is shaped by this perception of the inherent value of the human person." Ultimately, his vision also was grounded in the theological belief that all Christians, through baptism, are called to minister.

While bishop of Kansas City-St. Joseph, John gave numerous talks and wrote articles on his vision of lay ministry and how his experiences prior to becoming a bishop shaped his ideas. "The more I reflect on my experience with people, the more I am convinced that giving witness is always what unites them," he wrote in a February 1980 article in *Marriage and Family Living* magazine. "Perhaps my dream is really of people giving witness out of the wondrous power of the Spirit of God. Giving witness seems to be where my dream is at. And that makes it a dream of shared ministry, for giving witness is what ministry is about. . . .Giving witness is the vocation of every Christian. Baptism into the death and resurrection of Christ goes to the very core of a person. It calls us out of a purely human existence and into a living of the Christian life. . . . People need to be prepared to meet the ministerial responsibilities of giving the witness expected of them."

Grounded in spirituality

In a talk to lay ministers in Tulsa, Oklahoma, in November 1986, John noted, "I have personally learned a great deal since my ordination about what it means to minister. Ministry must be grounded in spirituality. Whether I am a clergyman, a medical professional, a pastoral care worker or a parish volunteer, I must be motivated by the Spirit of God. In days gone by, it seemed so simple because the Roman collar and the religious garb were the signs of the minister. He or she was the one who would give and someone else would receive the gifts of ministry. The older I become, the more I become aware that ministers are simultaneously 'receivers and givers.' The minister is not always identifiable. The real effective minister is one who is present and available to life and deeply in touch with the Lord."

George Noonan, who worked with John for nine years as director of the Center for Pastoral Life and Ministry in Kansas City, believes John's early work in mission dioceses and parishes helped him "stumble onto the importance of the laity. His heart has always been very much with the domestic missions, and you could really do something there with lay personnel. There are some bishops that only accept lay ministry because of the current lack of priests. Fundamentally, Bishop Sullivan, given his heart and experience, doesn't do that. But it has always intrigued me that he didn't set out to become a major spokesperson on the subject but rather a major doer. And through that he became a major spokesperson. . . . He has consistently had a deep concern for developing ministry in the church, and he expects quality and orthodoxy of those who work with him."

Sister Cele Breen, a member of the Sisters of Charity of Leavenworth, who had first met John in Grand Island, joined the Center's staff in 1984. "I never saw his (John's) vision as tied to a shortage of priests, but to his conviction that this is what baptism means," she says. "I don't know if I've ever heard him lay out his vision philosophically, but it's been shown more by where he's put the diocesan money, where he's stood behind things. It's really been more where he's placed the priorities and allowed things to happen." She says John was "convinced beyond any doubt that laypeople wanted to be trained. It wasn't just turning them loose on parishes. He wanted them educated, formed and supported, so much so that I think the priests in our diocese felt that he neglected them. But I know from talking to him that his vision is that they would all work together. . . . It was just recognizing the reality that you've got to have more people to work together in parishes."

Personal experience

John believes his recognition of the importance of lay ministry to the life of the church was not merely the result of theological reflection and dialogue, but of his many years of personal experience as a priest. He says also his vision was reinforced by the experience of Vatican II. Sociologically and historically, the fields of lay ministry had been plowed decades before Vatican II, John noted in a November 1990 talk. "The active involvement of the laity in this country has deep and strong roots. Now it is our own age and our responsibility to interpret and articulate theologically the importance and perdurable necessity of our broadened concept of ministry. In the 25 years since the close of the Council, we have been fortunate enough to experience much greater emphasis on the importance of the sacrament of baptism. . . . It is in baptism that each of us is called by God to share in the life and mission of the church. Lay ministry emerges naturally from a theology of church which stresses the call to holiness and service to others that all of us receive at baptism and for which each of us is given certain gifts . . . The council revealed that the sacrament of baptism, the sacraments of initiation, are the significant, primary sacraments."

Grasped Vatican II theology

Sister Rosemary Ferguson, Dominican Sister who directed the Center for Pastoral Life and Ministry in Kansas City from 1979-81, assesses that John "really grasped the theology of Vatican II." John "had that inner sense that the laity needed to be educated and they couldn't continue in an uninformed way. He made a big impression on me because he had that sense of the people. I was so impressed with the energy he had for providing good contemporary Vatican II theology for the laity."

"I have always thought John's vision arose out of Vatican II and his concept of how the laity would be active in the church and not just submissive," contends Jim Tierney, who served as John's diocesan attorney in Kansas City-St. Joseph. "Some of it came from his experience with Extension (Volunteers). He was aware early on of the problems of the diminishing number of priests and he also felt that women's talents were underutilized. And he sensed there was so much more to be done for the church out there, other than administering the sacraments, which only a priest could do. He thought it was appropriate to get the laity really involved in the ministerial work of the church. He also realized that lay

Catholics after World War II had educational advantages that they had not had before. And that they had an intelligent or more reasoning view of their faith. And it wasn't just based solely on tradition."

Noonan says John also saw the call to ministry as intimately tied to the meaning of the Eucharist. "He's a strong believer in the Eucharist," he notes. "And he sees it as a transformative experience; he doesn't see it as a passive one. And that transformative side says that you have to respond, you have to go out there and work the world and move the world along."

A call to serve

John stressed this idea particularly in a pastoral letter on the Eucharist, issued August 4, 1985. "No matter what changes take place in the church, the Eucharist continues to be the center of our faith life," he wrote. "The Eucharist is a call to serve, to minister to the Christian community and the world. . . . The Eucharist is not the prayer of the ordained clergy but of the whole eucharistic community that is gathered. Therefore, we should not be surprised, but encouraged by the presence of the variety of ministers in our parish. Ministry, however, does not simply reside only within the boundaries of the gathered community of the Eucharist. Each person gathered at the Eucharist is invited to live the Eucharist in the everyday times and surroundings of all of our lives."

And later, on his 10th anniversary as bishop of Kansas City-St. Joseph in 1987, John wrote, "The Eucharist is not out of the world. It is the heart of the world. It is a people giving thanks to God, who out of gratefulness, give back to God by serving other people in small ways and large."

John says as early as the mid-1960s he "dreamed of a place where the unique formation for lay ministry could be provided. I dreamed of a place where preparation for parish-based ministry would be offered for and made accessible to all baptized persons." The Center for Pastoral Life and Ministry in Kansas City was an attempt to respond to that dream. John was steadfast in his vision to form this nationally-known diocesan training center for ministry, even though he met resistance at times from some priests and laity within his own diocese.

"An early reaction by a lot of the priests was that they were threatened," recalls Father Richard Carney. "The reaction was, 'If we have all these ministers, what are we as priests going to do?' The talk among some of the priests was that they were simply going to be 'Mass priests,' we're going to be robots. It wasn't a large number of priests, but it was a considerable number that were not secure. And Bishop Sullivan explicitly mentioned men and women in ministry, so other priests who were of that bent might also be threatened by women. They weren't open to women taking principal places in ministry or administration. Nevertheless, people I associated with were very much supportive of his idea, especially after the bishop's vision statement in 1980, when it became more clear what his goals were."

Focus changed

Over the years, the focus of the Center for Pastoral Life and Ministry changed and evolved. John notes that this coincided with his own development in thinking that there must be a balance between ministry skills training and faith enrichment. In 1984, six years after it was started and when Noonan became director of the Center, its focus was on three areas to help ministerial development in the Kansas City-St. Joseph diocese. The first was to act as a resource for the parishes for adult education, whether it was through the staff or by suggesting other resources. The second was to work in the area of staff development with the parishes. This was a long-term involvement with the pastor, parish council and staff of a parish to establish a parish-based formative experience for parishioners called to ministry. The third area focused on training ministers through two tracks: a foundational program aimed at competency in ministry and cooperative projects with diocesan agencies and departments. The first track included the master's level program offered in cooperation with Loyola University of New Orleans. Also in this track was "New Wine," the diocesan formation for ministry program started in 1985.

John himself detailed the shift in focus over time of the Center in an interview on his 10th anniversary as bishop and in a talk on lay ministry in November 1988. "It has taken us a number of years to focus properly on the mission of the Center," he said in 1987. "Originally, the staff was called on for adult education programs in parishes. But now the programs are restricted very much to ministerial training and formation, faith enrichment of ministers, and program development in parishes. The Center's mission today is one that is tied to a realistic vision of what ministry will be in the church in the future."

"With any such attempt to bring dreams into reality, there was a period of, shall we call it, 'sleep walking,'" John admitted in the 1988 talk. "That's the time when you stumble, backtrack, and occasionally lose sight of what you hoped to accomplish in the first place." In working to bring the Center into place, he noted, there had been several "gaffs."

The first mistake was assuming that by running people through an intense ministry training program they would automatically be qualified as a minister in the church, he said. "This approach, which reduced ministry to formula skills training, completely negates the 'mystery' of faith and the sources of grace and belief from which ministry flows," he said. "How can we teach someone who is not in touch with his or her own faith life to talk openly and honestly to others about this faith? How can you train someone to represent Christ to the grieving, the alienated, the lonely when they themselves do not know Christ in their deepest hearts? How long will such people last without the internal strength of faith or the external support of the faith community?"

Growth in ministry

The "flip side" to this "gaff," John noted, was spiritual growth is not always the same as growth in ministry. "Unfortunately, one can be holy and still lack the competence to aid others in their spiritual search or assist them in meeting real, often dramatic, personal or material needs," he said. "In our zest to reinforce the relationship between faith and ministry, we run the danger of training ministers to do one thing well: for instance, to give adult retreats. There must be a balance between ministry skills and faith enrichment. The formula for such a balance must be continually monitored and adjusted by those charged with leadership in lay ministry development."

The third mistake was assuming there was an abundance of people available to train ministers, John said. "We soon learned that not everyone with an advanced degree in theology, pastoral psychology, adult education or religious education understands the concept of ministry, to say nothing of being able to provide training for it," he said. "Many of the people we interviewed could only perceive training in the 'academic' model, where the transferal of skills are measured and evaluated in testing situations. Moreover, we discovered that many of our prospective teachers felt removed from the parish situation — the situation where we wanted ministry developed. Some of our early attempts at ministry training began to look very much like Theology 401."

Underestimating the resistance to change evidenced by many of the parishes was the fourth mistake, John said. "Ministry in general, much less lay ministry, is a phenomenon not fully understood, much less embraced, by many parish communities. Educating for ministry is doomed unless there are corresponding attempts to prepare parish communities for accepting ministry. In this regard, I have learned the placement of priest personnel who understand and appreciate the nature of ministry into selected parishes is pivotal."

A final mistake John cited was separating the Center initially from the rest of the diocesan administration. "Certainly, there must be integrity in any formation program — the program must be free enough to respond to lay ministry needs as they occur and be separated enough from the 'status quo' to explore creative responses to current situations," John said. "However, just as ministry permeates the pastoral life of the local church, so also must it impact on the administration of that church on a day-to-day basis. The people who train ministers must be in contact with those charged with the ministry of leadership."

The reality of the Center, John concluded, is that it continues to be a place out of which training and support is provided for parish-based ministry. It approaches such training as "concurrent faith enrichment and skills development experience. In obtaining qualified staff, the Center now identifies individuals with experience and an understanding of the challenges of ministry. If that person does not have the 'academic' credentials, then we invest in that person and send him or her to school to acquire those credentials."

Let people develop

John "entered the diocese when the diocesan pastoral council was dying and he never did anything to restore it," reflects George Noonan. "He never gave the Center a mandate with pastoral councils. But again, maybe that was saying something — that to mandate things would perhaps kill them in the long run. Maybe this has been the better way — let people develop, let them fight their battles, and then you will get something that will last. He wanted people to use the Center and it bothered him that some people didn't use it, but he never mandated the Center. So maybe there's something instinctual about that, and that fundamentally maybe that will make it last. The test is ahead of us.

"Ultimately, I think Bishop Sullivan's vision of lay ministry will prove itself out," Noonan adds. "The best interpretation of him is that he is a product of his time and culture.

With lay ministry he was getting there, but also still struggling along."

"The diocesan priests over time have been more accepting of the Center," John notes. "We have to say, 'What if we didn't have it?' I'm an optimistic person anyway, but if we didn't have the Center, as far as I'm concerned, we'd be in trouble. Even more so now than when we started it."

"The Center, even to this day, may be a noble experiment that fails, but it is indeed a noble experiment," contends Father Patrick Rush, now diocesan vicar general. "I think that's where a lot of Bishop Sullivan's strengths lie. And if only half or part of his vision amounts to something, that's a lot. Being a visionary, he was on the cutting edge and there was not a lot of precedent for programs. They may or may not be all that effective. That's not a criticism of them. A lesser bishop wouldn't have thought of them and wouldn't have tried them."

Long-term results

Some of the long-term results of the work of the Center for Pastoral Life and Ministry are the New Wine program (recently published by Paulist Press and a national model for lay ministry formation), the implementation of the Rite of Christian Initiation of Adults in most parishes and the high caliber of parish staffs in the diocese. New Wine, started in 1985, is a 30-month program of education and formation to prepare people for lay ministry, led by the staff of the Center. It requires courses in Scripture, church history, theology, morality, sacraments, church law and doctrine, liturgy, prayer and worship, leadership and human development. To date, 137 people have completed New Wine.

The numbers who have finished New Wine are "deceptive," says Noonan. "There's some dioceses that could have produced hundreds more during these years. But that's our whole point. We're not in it for the numbers, we're in it for the quality and the development of each person. I'm not going to pretend that everyone who goes through New Wine, just as not everyone who goes through the seminary, comes out as the best candidate for ministry. New Wine is about formation, not cloning. But I think we've developed a good program that would have been impossible to develop without Bishop Sullivan's support. A lot of his support was just letting us figure it out. When he trusts you, he leaves you to develop something."

Sister Cele, who has been involved with New Wine since its inception, notes John has been proud of the program because "he never intended to just throw lay ministers out into parishes without them having the formation they needed. The hard part about New Wine is that after they complete the program and go back to the parishes, these people are then seen sometimes as a threat to the priests . . . I don't think we've reached even halfway up the hill yet. We've always had the advantage of knowing that Bishop Sullivan was behind us."

Lots of people involved

Brother Michael Fehrenbach, now coordinator of New Wine, says the lay ministry that John has nurtured in Kansas City-St. Joseph bodes well for the future of the diocese. "We've got lots of people involved," he says. "These are people who have a deeper understanding of what the church calls them to do than they would have had if he hadn't been here. I'm not saying he was the only one who could have done it. But he was the one who was here, and who gave us the impetus."

Father Michael Roach, now pastor of St. Patrick's Parish in north Kansas City, says a major accomplishment of the Center and New Wine is many parishes with high quality staffs. "I think that's due to Bishop Sullivan's 'hands off' approach," he says. "He wasn't somebody sitting in judgment and calling us to task, but he let us have the freedom to develop and to do what we felt we needed to do in our parishes. And he supported us and I appreciated it. I think he was very proud of the Center and how he let it develop."

Another longtime dream of John's regarding lay ministry was realized in the establishment of the Institute for Pastoral Life (IPL) in 1985. This national center for lay ministry training was funded by the Catholic Church Extension Society. John co-founded the IPL with several other home mission bishops, including Bishop William Friend of Shreveport, Louisiana, and Bishop Ricardo Ramirez of Las Cruces, New Mexico. During the seven years it operated out of St. John's Diocesan Center in Kansas City, the institute drew national attention for educating and energizing lay ministers to serve in priest-short areas. The impetus for the IPL can be traced to John's "concept paper" for a national training center for lay volunteers, written in April 1966 while he was director of the Extension Volunteers. The IPL's mission statement noted that the institute was especially attentive to the multicultural dimension of the U.S. church, to the home mission and smaller dioceses, to places facing the challenges of fewer priests, and particularly to parishes without a resident pastor.

Proper skills

John, who was president of the IPL's board of directors, knew that laypeople could not minister without the proper skills, contends Jean Marie Hiesberger, former director of the IPL. "Because he believed in quality formation, he knew it would take a long time to develop the institute," she says. "He wanted to get it done before there was a crisis." The beauty of John's vision, she adds, was that very few of the trained lay ministers from the IPL served in his own diocese. "It was never a self-interest enterprise," she says. "He was thinking of the bigger church. His own experience with the Center for Pastoral Life and Ministry was that it should be done for others as well, and there was a call in him that if he could make it happen, he should."

Initially, John saw the institute as training pastoral administrators to serve in priestless parishes, Hiesberger recalls, but she was unable to get any dioceses to commit to sending any pastoral administrators. ˙John "was for several years pushing me — why aren't you doing pastoral administrators?" she says. "And I would do survey after survey with bishops asking, 'If we had a summer program, how many would you send?' I'd have a grand total of seven or something. I think this was always a frustration for Bishop Sullivan, because he knew the need was out there and he really wanted us to work with pastoral administrators." Eventually IPL programs were designed to form pastoral leaders for parish communities without a resident pastor and to train diocesan directors of lay ministry from various dioceses to develop their own lay ministry programs of formation and education. Summer institutes were offered for the training and continuing education of religious, deacons and laity called to pastoral leadership in parishes.

A *similar vision*

Bishop Friend, who served with John on the IPL's board of directors, says, "we shared a similar vision that we needed to help the mission churches with the obvious priest shortage that they faced. It had been his experience with the Extension Volunteers and my experience in the Bible Belt that when priests are no longer available, you see the Catholic population suffer greatly in that area for leadership. And sometimes you have a loss of members." John had "great confidence in the ability of the laity, because he saw what they had done in the volunteer program — their competence, skills and great faith commitment. This made it easier for him than his brother bishops to invest heavily in the laity to be church and do the work of the church. . . . One of the disappointments of IPL for him and all of us was that we could not get some of the mission dioceses on board fast enough — they were slow and cautious. Some of it was because they didn't have the financial resources to invest in people."

The need for evangelization was at the heart of John's vision for the IPL, "and in order to evangelize, you need evangelizers," says Bishop Walter F. Sullivan of Richmond, Virginia, who also served on the board of directors. "When he (John) established the IPL, I don't believe the shortage of priests was all that apparent, but obviously he was sort of a prophet ahead of his time. . . . The church in the U.S. has always operated out of the mode of large dioceses with a heavy concentration of Catholics. For us in the South and in mission areas, that is simply a myth — we are very different. So new, imaginative approaches need to be made. John was a man of imagination who mixed it with a wealth of practical experience."

Theological questions

Some bishops were threatened by the possible development of pastoral administrators by the IPL, Hiesberger says. "The whole experience was very new. Even now, there are bishops very skeptical, if not at least tentative about the whole process. And the more it developed, the more theological questions began to come up. So there was an immediate dealing with additional issues, and we had a symposium for bishops." IPL's efforts eventually were not so much focused on pastoral administrators but on "the whole system of alternative ministry leadership," Hiesberger says.

"Quite frankly," Hiesberger adds, "I think early on there developed a backlash. And certain bishops set up a dichotomy that pitted priests against lay administrators; if you're for lay administrators, you're anti-cleric."

Bishop Friend adds, "It was a reality that John's emphasis on lay ministry caused some bishops to have a great concern that if the laity were enabled as a parish life coordinator or pastoral administrator, we would weaken the church's effort to foster vocations to the priesthood and undermine the efforts of the ordained priest. On the other side of the spectrum, all of us received criticism from arch-liberals who said that what we were attempting would inhibit or at

least complicate efforts to have married clergy and women's
ordination. We were in a 'buzzsaw' situation of getting criticism from both sides of the spectrum.

Handled both sides

"I thought John handled this very well as chair of the
IPL board," Bishop Friend adds. "He could address both
sides of the issue. In all situations, when you believe that
you are acting in the right intention, have a solid theological
base, and are trying to do the right thing to help the church,
you just keep walking in that direction. That's what John
did . . . Unfortunately, some of the bishops' concerns, when
voiced in a forceful manner, sometimes undermined (Extension's) financing of the IPL."

Nothing would deter John from continuing to try and
convince people of the importance of the IPL for the church's
long-term benefit, Hiesberger contends. "It didn't matter
that the bishops weren't supporting this; it didn't matter that
we didn't have enough money. He told me it still needs to be
done, so just figure out how to do it," she recalls. "It was
difficult for Bishop Sullivan to comprehend why other bishops didn't understand. It was just as clear as day to him
how we needed to train people, because he was looking into
the future and they were looking to the end of the day, as it
were . . . I always thought he was an idealist, but he also
operates out of a very pragmatic vision that if we don't take
certain steps, we're walking away from our future. We're not
going to have a future if we don't have people to do ministry.
For him it wasn't a matter of priests or laypeople, it was we
need somebody doing ministry. He showed remarkable patience when you think about how many years he lived with
this and kept on and on."

There was a difference of opinion about how to present
the IPL to donors of the Extension Society, Hiesberger says.
"Bishop Sullivan's view was that the donors could be educated and that this is something that they could really get

enthused about, if we would be allowed to present it to them," she notes. "And we could win their hearts by focusing on the people in the mission areas."

The IPL closed in Kansas City on April 30, 1992 for financial reasons, as the Extension Society was no longer able to sustain the project as it had in the past, and the dioceses served were unable to provide such projects for themselves because of their financial limitations. In its seven years of existence, the IPL trained 45 diocesan directors of ministry, who took a 300-hour course and were able to train others for ministry in their own dioceses. The IPL's summer institute for diocesan-designated leaders in parishes without resident priests trained another 240 people. The institute sponsored four national symposia and published 13 books and videotapes. Through a training program in the Diocese of Shreveport, Louisiana, the IPL trained another 58 people in a 20-week parish life enhancement program. Although the institute is still alive on the campus of Loyola University in New Orleans, it is down to a part-time director and a handful of programs, Hiesberger says.

The IPL has often been described as an idea slightly ahead of its time. "The aim of the IPL to help home mission dioceses and parishes deal with the changes in parish ministry is still the challenge of the larger church as well," says Bishop Ricardo Ramirez, chairman of the board of the IPL when it closed. "The demise of the IPL might be due to the fact that other bishops just weren't at the same place yet as John in his understanding of training for lay ministers. He was ahead of everyone else."

"I don't think the IPL was a failure at all," concludes John. "The ending was a disappointment. But what happened with the people who were trained was not a failure. Something like the IPL is needed more than ever. I feel the whole experience was just a chapter in the whole evolution of pastoral ministry."

CHAPTER NINE

The Legacy of John J. Sullivan

TOO OFTEN CATHOLICS TEND TO VIEW THE CHURCH AS THE Vatican or the diocesan chancery office instead of what it really is: the corporate body of Christ, with a unity created and sustained by the Holy Spirit. This is the first and most basic ecclesiological principle taught by the Second Vatican Council — that the church is a mystery or sacrament and not only or even primarily an institution or organization. And this is the principle which guided the ministry of John Sullivan as priest, pastor and bishop, as he tried to manifest visibly what the church embodies invisibly.

As John noted in his "Vision" statement in 1980, he believed his common vision for the local church could be actualized because he recognized the "unique mystery" of the church. "Ultimately, my belief in the attainability of these dreams and goals stems from our shared faith," he said. "We need continually to remind ourselves that the church is not a mere human enterprise, but a mystery. . . . We cannot think of the church as an institution, a human corporation, into which we infuse the abstraction of mystery. For us, the church is real — it is a real, historic, happening-in-this-day, a happening-in-this-hall event."

Most real about John's ministry was his ability to give hope to people of faith, whether lay, religious or ordained. Wherever and whenever he has been able to "pastor," he has touched people's lives. John "wanted to provide people with quality pastoral care — that's the bottom line," says Archbishop Thomas J. Murphy of Seattle, who worked with John on the board of the Institute for Pastoral Life. "His ministry was one that responded to concrete needs and enabled him to speak to the heart. . . . The wonderful thing about John Sullivan is that he has a real religious sensitivity that is incarnational — it is the hand to touch human life."

"I experienced John's approach to ministry as very forward-looking, focused on what the church ought to be doing in a community — the service people should give and the witness they should offer," notes Bishop John Leibrecht of Springfield, Missouri. "John is innately pastoral. He doesn't know how to be any other way. It came so naturally that if he hadn't become a priest, he would have found some other way to identify with people and be concerned about them. . . . I think his pastoral sense predated his becoming a priest, and it was the same spirit with which he ministered in parishes before he became a bishop."

In many ways, John continued his pastoral work as a bishop. But it was also a sacrifice because he loved being a parish priest and relating to people on that basis. He often felt loneliness "at the top." "If I were isolated, I couldn't function. Now that may just be a 'flaw in my character,' a personality trait, but it's real for me," he said in an interview with *The Catholic Key* on his 10th anniversary in Kansas City-St. Joseph.

Availability of a bishop

"The availability of a bishop is so important. You are not dealing with an abstract population, but you're dealing with people where they live — with their heartaches, joys and loves — where their needs are. I just love people, and I try to relate to them in a personal way. This availability to people seems to be a necessary characteristic for a bishop in today's church. It has an awful lot to do with being pastoral . . . the feeling of being close to people. But when you give this much to people, you do leave yourself open to some suffering."

Sister Annie Hilger, a Sister of the Sorrowful Mother from Broken Arrow, Oklahoma, lived and worked with John (as his secretary and later as his housekeeper) from 1973 to 1989 in Grand Island and Kansas City. "I always thought Bishop Sullivan would much rather be a parish priest at times," she recalls. "He said many times how much he really missed being in a parish. But he also knew the responsibilities of being a bishop and took them very seriously. I always knew there was a good reason why he had those broad shoulders — he had a lot of burdens to carry."

John always "had a vision of what church should be. He was a dreamer and people-oriented, and had that spirit of evangelizing," says Sister Mary Helen McInerney, who has known John since he was pastor of St. Mary's Church in Guthrie. "In Grand Island, he would drive up to a rectory wearing his lumber jacket. He was not pretentious at all. I think, however, after he became a bishop, he became a little more cautious. Because of the role of bishop he lost a little of the spontaneity. I thought that the office of bishop sometimes prevented him from being able to show his feelings, but the spirit of concern for people was there." Says Father John Schuele, "Occasionally, I would get the sense from Bishop Sullivan that it's lonely at the top. In his job, he was constantly going to 'command performances.' I had the impression that being the bishop was the big leagues and playing minor league ball is just more fun."

The responsibilities of being a bishop "were like a cross and ropes that entangled Bishop Sullivan from what he really wanted to do," contends Neal Colby, Catholic Charities director in Kansas City. "I remember being with him at a series of meetings and he leaned over to me and said, 'Meetings, meetings — I know I'm going to die at a meeting.' He hated what got in the way of his being a pastoral bishop and being with people. Being a bishop was a great sacrifice on his part."

Shepherd and pastor

Throughout his ministry, John reflected "being shepherd and pastor," assesses Father Gerald Waris. "He was very open and accepting of people. Some would say he lived the pluralism of the church. There was room for everyone and he kept the door open. It was very difficult for him to make the tough decisions; it was heart-wrenching for him. I was witness to some of those and they pained him a great deal. There's the side of justice and there's the side of forgiveness. There's the side of administration and there's the side of pastoring. All those play against each other as bishop, and they moved in and out of his heart frequently."

An enduring belief for John, nurtured from his years as a pastor, was the right of lay Catholics to be educated in pastoral and theological issues. "I always felt we were going to reap the evils of tolerating illiteracy in religious education among our people," John says. "I was convinced that formation and training were absolutely necessary. I could accept that change was slow, but sometimes it was unnecessarily slow."

John's conviction about pastoral education was the impetus behind his ideas of the team ministry in the Grand Island diocese, the Center for Pastoral Life and Ministry in Kansas City, and the Institute for Pastoral Life, contends Jean Marie Hiesberger. "The education piece is really a part of his pastoring vision. You can't pastor without good formation. And you need to attend to the formation in a serious way so that the pastoring can take place. His experiences convinced him of all this," she says.

Necessity of ministerial formation

John summarized his thoughts in part in an address at the Bishop's Recognition Dinner before several hundred people on Feb. 14, 1988. "I cannot exaggerate the importance and necessity of ministerial formation and education in the faith for all who will fill ministry roles in the future," he noted. "The main focus of our efforts must be at the parish level where our people live and struggle.

"Our parishes will need stable, trained professional leaders, many of whom will be non-ordained. The only option to utilizing the skills and talents of the non-ordained would be the ordination of women and married men. While this option is viewed by some as radical, we must realize that the most radical thing we could do is nothing at all — to have no plan for the future. These pastoral leaders may not be trained in seminaries, but they must be trained. . . . We are committed to the education of our parish leaders — a commitment we must maintain."

Father Patrick Rush believes John's vision of church was a pragmatic one that resulted from his own ministry experiences. "Bishop Sullivan probably was a visionary in part because he was so sensitive to the issues of people," he says. "His vision was fueled by people's experiences. His primary theological trainer was not the theory of the church but the experience of the church. In that sense he was amazing — he has an innate methodology to reflect upon his experience as a pastor. And out of that reflection evolved a vision that became his theology for the church, his agenda for the church. I don't think there are many people gifted at that type of reflective process."

Leadership style

Many who know John say his leadership style was inspired by a true understanding of people and a keen ability to evaluate people's talents and skills. Many contend he has been able to bring out the best in people — especially those who worked for him as a bishop — because of his great faith and trust in them. John, reflecting on his own style, notes, "I might have had more confidence in laypeople than some other bishops did. If you're going to inhibit or restrict people, it just won't work. . . . Over the years, I have been fortunate in screening and hiring people. . . . I found people to whom I could give responsibilities and then placed my trust in them."

Jim Tierney, diocesan attorney in Kansas City-St. Joseph who worked with John for more than 15 years, says, "This may be my prejudice, but I don't think I know anybody else in the business world who was better in evaluating people's talents and putting the right people in the right slots. . . . I'm sure he had encouragement in various ways but those personnel decisions were his. He also knew and understood the weaknesses of his people."

John expected much from his staff, particularly in service to people, contends George Noonan. At the same time, he trusted his staff to stay on course in terms of quality and orthodoxy. "That's supportive because it allows you to work effectively," Noonan says. "When someone trusts you, you try to honor that trust. . . . Even in the nine years we worked together, I can't say at what point I knew things had clicked between us — where the trust was. I guess I always felt I had it or somewhere along the way I earned it. But he (John) never made me feel like I had to earn it. You just try to work hard, try to move things in the right direction, try to respond to your gut feeling. And he's supportive of you."

Maureen Kelly, who worked with John both in Grand Island (as diocesan director of religious education) and in Kansas City-St. Joseph (on the staff of the Center), says John influenced her ministry because he involved women in decision-making. "When my office proposed something, I was supported; I was listened to," she recalls. "Bishop Sullivan was very collaborative; he really respected me personally and did not pull in the reigns on what I wanted to do. . . . He created a place of freedom and openness. He knows how to get good people to map out strategy. But he expected you to be a self-starter, to initiate and move ahead."

John had the ability to lay out a broad picture and then find people who could fill in the details for implementing it, contends Sister Judy Warmbold, who has known John since the team ministry effort in the Grand Island diocese.

"Bishop Sullivan's personal charism played a big part," she says. "He recruits people who can do the job, and once they're on board he doesn't always have to be around. He has the ability to spot talent and then give people enough freedom to do their jobs. He totally relies on you."

Adds Sister Cele Breen, who worked with John throughout his years in Kansas City-St. Joseph, "Bishop Sullivan's had this vision, but I don't know that it's always well-articulated. What he had was the ability to get people who could translate the vision into something. . . . Maybe that's his whole idea with collaborative ministry and it's a part of him — that you turn things over, you delegate. You have to put confidence in people. I don't know that he would articulate that, but that's what it is. His experience as a pastor in Guthrie was so crucial to what he believed about this."

Noonan describes John as "not a 'detail person' on many things — he's not one to say this is how it will happen. He knows what the picture looks like and he wants to get there. And he trusts other people to work out the details. He's sincere about what he says about the priesthood of all believers. He lives that in a genuine way. There are many who say those words because they make for nice platitudes, but don't really believe them."

Future role of priesthood

John's experiences as a priest and bishop have left him with definite ideas about the future role of the priesthood, as well as the qualities a bishop should possess in today's church. "The evolution into a new era of church leaves us with some very real and perplexing questions," John commented in an address in February 1986. "As a bishop in today's church, I am forced to ask some of these questions myself, and still other questions like these are brought to me: What is ministry? What are these multiple ministries? How do I develop a collegial leadership style and be less autocratic? How do I learn to work collaboratively in this ministry of evangelizing the world? What is the role of priest? How do men and women, ordained and non-ordained, learn to work together closely?

"These questions are not philosophical or theological questions, they are real, experiential questions arising from the experience of people in the church today," he added. "They deeply touch my life and other human lives and have an impact on them."

John said that while priests were trained once to be "lone rangers," today they must learn to enable, facilitate and coordinate a pastoral staff. "In the future, I personally see the priest as looking more like a 'mini-bishop.' His role will be expanded, not diminished. This ordained minister must realize it is the kingdom of Jesus that he is working at and not his own kingdom. . . . Sometimes the woman minister or the lay minister is criticized because he or she is fulfilling a role formerly filled by an ordained priest. We must learn to work with and try to understand these feelings experienced by ministers in today's church."

"We are still struggling with the role and nature of the priesthood in very changing times," John says today. "I see priests in the future having a greater emphasis on preparation in ministry, Scripture, theology and liturgy. We need to support them and build up morale because what is required of them today is heroic.

"There are many laypeople who are competent to take over the administrative tasks," he adds. "The reality is we are a eucharistic church, a sacramental church, and we have to have an ordained ministry. But in many places, leaders are in a state of denial, ignoring the realities of the median age of priests today and how few men are preparing for the priesthood. We don't seem to recognize the vocation crisis and the exodus from religious life we've experienced in the last 25 years. . . . Even if current trends are reversed tomorrow, it will take a long time to turn things around. And it's already having a profound impact on church life."

One of the key roles a bishop can play today is as servant, John says. "Two ways in which you serve as bishop are by your availability and your willingness to be with your priests, religious and laypeople. This is always what I meant about not becoming isolated. . . . What a bishop really needs is faith. He has to be courageous, and that is having an extraordinary trust in the Lord. A bishop has to foster trust. That's what makes him courageous. Most important, you have to be open and honest. You don't have to broadcast your every thought, but just be open and honest. If you don't do this, it's hopeless. You have to live your faith and witness to your faith. The only way people are going to be exposed to the truth sometimes is by the quality of your witness.

"I have never taken myself too seriously as far as my role in the church — you just have to do your best," John adds. "What you have to do is be open to the Spirit. There's risk involved if you try some new things, but there's even risk involved if you don't try. . . . Everything you do has to be taken with the awareness that what we're involved in is not a human enterprise, but working with the mystery of the church. And everything is possible if we trust in the Lord."

A model of leadership

Many people use "pastoral" to describe a style of being bishop, but it is not always clear what they mean. The term many times applies to a bishop who gets out of the office, visits parishes, and enjoys meeting people. In John's case, pastoral meant not only these qualities but a bishop who put the Catholic faith in the language of the people he served, who related to people's struggles. His was a model of pastoral leadership in some very difficult contemporary times in the American church. And many agree that such models of leadership are needed as the church enters the 21st century.

"The best leaders use stories and symbols to relate to people. And Bishop Sullivan is a master user of stories," contends Jim Tierney. "He has said — and I think it's accurate — that he considers himself a worker and not a theorist or great thinker. In his years in Kansas City-St. Joseph, there has been tension between Catholics who wanted things to stay the way they were before Vatican II and Catholics who were truly post-Vatican II. I think his goal was to make that tension fruitful. Out of that tension — both permitting it and not letting it get out of hand — there has been real progress made in the faith of people."

John was "not absolutist or single-minded," Tierney adds. "He recognized that as you came up with answers as a result of resolving tensions, that each answer posed new questions and created new tensions, none of which could be easily resolved. He accepted that as the way the church ought to progress. He favored a conciliatory approach. He recognized that growth in the church requires not a repudiation of the core beliefs, but extreme care and resourcefulness in shaping the core beliefs and building on them. His own personal faith was conservative, and he was able to distinguish between the core and the peripheral beliefs. . . . When a great leader's work is done, the people say, 'We did it ourselves.' That's Bishop Sullivan's style of leadership and that was his desire."

John's personality allowed him to interact with liberal and conservative Catholics alike and helped him to teach both groups, says George Noonan. "It's been proven over the years — there's no doubt the man has a vision. It's a vision that cannot totally escape who he is and how he has been formed. So that's always a counterbalancing tension within Bishop Sullivan. His greatest accomplishments, especially in lay ministry, were letting things develop, supporting them, and not getting too panicky. . . . There are many other bishops that might have been in the public eye articulating different positions, whether for lay ministry or other things. But Bishop Sullivan basically didn't waste his time with words, he worked out his beliefs and acted.

"One of Bishop Sullivan's advantages was that in his career he saw the church from many angles — the Chicago and East Coast hierarchy, the mission territory, the Midwest. He didn't have a speculative theory of ministry but a very formative one. He's no liberal, although he has been perceived as such. I call him moderately progressive."

Father John Schuele describes John's presence as a bishop as "authoritative, but never authoritarian. I never saw him shake his finger at anyone. He was authoritative because he was in touch, because he was oriented to the future. You could never separate the substance of the issues from the substance of the man. His sense of personal style really facilitated a lot of decisions. . . . If you were in a meeting, you knew everyone was going to hear what was on his mind that day. We all laughed about this. But I think it gave people a sense of some kind of inclusiveness. He didn't operate in a vacuum; he seemed to operate out of conviction. I probably won't know for years how much an impact he's had on me. I never agreed with him on everything, but that's not the point. We could always talk and he was open to my ideas. He was always forward-looking. He had a knack for not getting stuck in one place. And that's a gift."

John stands out as one of the visionary bishops of the latter part of this century, contends Bishop Ricardo Ramirez of Las Cruces, New Mexico. "Behind his jovial spirit and his openness is a very serious love and concern for all things church. He eats, breathes and exudes church. He is so life-giving. Every time I am with him, I go away a better bishop.

"John has been concerned about the whole mission of the church, perhaps more than any other bishop I know," concludes Bishop Ramirez. "He has a missionary spirit, based on his love of the church. He loves the church so much that he wants everyone to belong. That has been the passion of his ministry."

Postscript Reflection

AN IMPORTANT INTERVIEW THAT IS MISSING FROM THIS BIOGRA-
phy is one that Julie Sly had planned to conduct with my
close friend, Archbishop John L. May, who died this year after a 20-month fight with brain cancer. Unfortunately,
because of his illness, he was unable to offer his reflections
on our ministry together.

John May died at 11:50 p.m. on March 24, 1994, just 10
minutes before the feast of the Annunciation and what would
have been the 14th anniversary of his installation as Archbishop of St. Louis. We had known each other since 1959,
when he was named general secretary and vice president of
the Catholic Church Extension Society. He later served as
president of the society from 1967 to 1970, before becoming
bishop of the newly-created Diocese of Mobile, Alabama.

In his homily at John May's funeral Mass, Cardinal
(Joseph) Bernardin of Chicago said John's simple approach to
life "freed him from pretense or guile . . . enabled him to
speak very directly and clearly . . . did not require any external mask or ornamentation. And yet, despite his quiet, unas-
suming way, he made a tremendous impact on people. It
was not necessary that he speak a great deal to reveal himself and his love for others. There was a transparency in
him that enabled people quickly to see his goodness and his
spirituality."

I was extremely fortunate to share in that goodness and
spirituality for more than 30 years. Much of what is dis-

cussed in this book might have remained just ideas, or what John May called "a shimmering mirage," without his insightful, sometimes difficult, but always helpful challenges. I owe him a debt of gratitude. John May was a witness to the apostles. He has indeed gone before us to prepare a place for us.

Bishop John J. Sullivan
September 1994